Everyone has to cope with problems . . .

even such saints as Amy Carmichael, C.S. Lewis,
Charles Spurgeon and Hudson Taylor! These four
giants of the Christian faith faced their problems and, in
coping with them, increased their self-acceptance and
their Christian stature. They magnified the Lord Jesus
Christ in their lifetime and to succeeding generations.

Coping

Insights from:

Amy Carmichael
C.S. Lewis
Charles Spurgeon
Hudson Taylor

Elizabeth Skoglund

Regal Books A Division of G/L Publications
Ventura, California, U.S.A.

To Lois Curley
who shares my delight
in this particular selection of people
from that larger "cloud of witnesses."

Scripture quotations in this publication are from the Authorized King James Version; also quoted is *The Emphasized Bible,* Translation by James Joseph Rotherham, Cincinnati: The Standard Publishing Co., 1897, and *The Living Bible,* copyright © 1971 by Tyndale House Publishers, Wheaton, Illinois. Used by permission.

Fourth Printing, 1980

Published by Regal Books Division
A Division of G/L Publicatons
Ventura, California 93006
Printed in U.S.A.

Library of Congress Catalog Card No. 79-65538
ISBN 0-8307-0727-1

CONTENTS

CHAPTER 1
Coping in a
Tension Filled World

As I lay in a hammock overlooking the deep blue waters of the Zihuatanejo Bay, I felt I could cope with anything. The hot tropical sun was at its afternoon peak but I was shielded from it by a large tree with enormous leaves. Looking out over the water was an experience of sheer tranquility. Up and down the beach I could see singular figures at various places, napping, reading or just resting under shelter from the sun.

My body relaxed in the afternoon heat. No deadlines pressed in on me. No telephone was available if someone had wanted to reach me. No appointments were written into my purse-size date book. It was the closest I had come in a long time to the eradication of all pain. No pressure. No worry. No irritation. Yet when I remembered that in the morning I would have to get up early and catch a plane to Mexico City and then home, I knew with a twinge of sadness that I had not eradicated pain. All the pressures of ordinary life would undoubtedly be waiting when I arrived home. But I had refurbished my strength and developed a greater ability to cope.

In contrast to many of our misconceptions regarding life and our tendency to focus on happiness and the eradication of pain, Dr. Joseph Fabry states his views simply and concisely in the context of logotherapy, a therapy of meaning. Says Fabry:

"What I gained from logotherapy is the recognition that central to man's life is the pursuit of meaning, and not the pursuit of happiness; that we only invite frustration if we expect life to be primarily pleasurable; that life imposes obligations, and that pleasure and happiness come from responding to the tasks of life."

In this statement by Dr. Fabry, and indeed in the writings of Dr. Viktor Frankl who developed the ideas of logotherapy, several concepts are clear. Life focuses on coping, not eradicating. We have not been promised a rose garden; but then we have not been set down in the midst of thorns either. Realistically, we see life as having both pain and pleasure, with the pain kept minimal by our coping ability.

From this vantage point we will cease to berate ourselves for being so unspiritual as to suffer. Instead, we will accept God's gift of joy and even find happiness in living lives content in a task. Sometimes meaning will be found, not lost, in suffering. For although we try by all means to avoid pain, there are times when it cannot be eradicated. Then the best solution to that pain is to find some meaning in it.

In real life only children believe that pain always goes away; and even they learn quickly that such is not the case. Only the insane achieve in actuality the eradication of all pain; and they do it by denying reality, not finding it.

In this century and in this country we look upon happiness and freedom from pain as inalienable rights, the reward for a person who manages his life well. Our worship of pleasure feeds this. So does our distorted view of the "normal Christian life." We easily become disillusioned with our lives. We forget what Christ told us that in this life we would have sorrow. We quote verses referring to the joy of God without defining the word "joy." We forget the ups and downs, the delights and despair of the psalmist David. And we often forget that even in all of David's distress of mind and anguish of soul, he was the one described in Scriptures as a man after God's own heart.

In contrast to the current barrage of literature which promises fast answers, instant success and unending happiness to those who read and follow, earlier figures in Christian thinking promised no such things. But what they did offer was realistic and it worked.

Charles Haddon Spurgeon, the "prince of preachers" in nineteenth-century England, had little hope to offer those who wished to eradicate depression. Battling his own periodic times of deep distress, he had much good counsel on how to cope with and even positively use the problem of depression. I have read nothing since the writings of Spurgeon which, on a psychological and spiritual level, handles the subject more aptly.

Amy Wilson Carmichael, founder of the Dohnavur

mission in India, also wrote eloquently on a number of subjects; but with particular insight on the problem of suffering. Again firm realism: suffering cannot be eliminated from life. Yet in no way did Amy Carmichael feel that God allows us to be tossed around by the whim of fate, as we try hopelessly to escape suffering. Neither does she propose that we lie down helplessly under its power. Like Spurgeon, she presents practical help and realistic suggestions that can build hope and meaning in relationship to suffering.

Founder of the China Inland Mission, Hudson Taylor knew that God does not eliminate need. But instead of employing cheap methods in order to support his work, he discovered a great principle of the Christian life: God's work, done in God's way, will receive God's supply. And it worked not only for Hudson Taylor in China, but for George Müller and his orphanages in England and for Amy Carmichael in her work with children dedicated to the gods in South India.

More contemporary but certainly untainted by the froth of Christian thought, C.S. Lewis had enough strength to face and declare that humanness cannot be eradicated and that it is indeed not sinful. Some things are not black and white. There are varying shades of gray. Humanness is one of these. It can be coped with and even improved, but not eradicated.

Eradication is unrealistic. Coping is truthful and therefore is more likely to work. We hide the truth from ourselves and others if we deny this. Not too long ago I was on a talk show with a man who directed a Christian organization. At the outset this man turned to the talk show host and said: "I have never felt anger since the day I became a Christian."

The host turned to me and laughed, "Then we're in for an interesting show since you just wrote a book on anger!"

The show went on, and several questions were directed to me about my book, *To Anger, With Love*. The idea of our conflict on the subject did not come up until the end of the two-hour show when my friend said vehemently: "You know, I got *so* angry at Satan!"

There was a dead silence and then a roar of laughter from the talk show host. Even my friend here had not eradicated anger. He just hoped he had and had tried to make himself believe that he had succeeded. He viewed eradication, not coping, as the solution to life's problems.

As children, and even as adults, we try hard to eliminate unpleasant emotions from our lives. Sometimes we try so fervently that we even believe we have succeeded until we are jolted back into reality by the obvious recurrence of those feelings. But in actuality, all feelings—pleasant as well as unpleasant—are part of life. The great challenge is to use them and to grow through them, to control them. For it is in the contrast between pain and pleasure that both emotions are really felt; and it is in their tension and conflict that we often grow.

In a sense, the tranquility of the Zihuatanejo Bay would have been flat and lifeless had it not been experienced in contrast to the tension of life. The relaxation alone would not have reenergized me. It would have lulled me into a deadly depression, leading to emptiness, not to a task.

CHAPTER 2

Coping with Depression

An Insight into the Life
of Charles Spurgeon

"If I were a better Christian I wouldn't get so depressed" is a common statement from twentieth-century Christians when they feel discouraged or experience deep disappointment. Such an attitude may be fostered by some Christian literature that seems to equate depression with a lack of faith. Well-intentioned friends urge those who are depressed to "claim God's promises and be happy."

"God is the only tranquilizer I need," claimed one listener when she telephoned in on a TV talk show where I was a guest. This is by no means the first time I have heard this concept expressed. Apparently, "pray, and your problems will disappear" continues as a popular idea in some Christian circles. Perhaps some forget that we Christians are human. Forgiven, yes—but still living within our humanity. We cannot be up, up, up all the time. A contrary view is neither scriptural nor tenable. Nobody can live on a continuing emotional high, for life comes inevitably equipped with valleys as well as mountaintops.

God does not promise that our faith will free us from all discouragement and conflict, but He does promise that the peace and power of His Spirit will give us the kind of joy that enables us to weather any afflictions of the body, mind and spirit. Amy Carmichael underscores this promise when she quotes H.W. Webb-Peploe's definition of Christian joy as that quiet, inner contentment that results from "perfect acquiescence in God's will." [1]

People in biblical times were certainly not always living on a spiritual high, nor did they attempt to use God as a giant tranquilizer to obliterate their difficulties. Neither did they scoff at nor condemn as "unspiritual" those who were hurting.

We in the twentieth century too often consider suffering to be synonymous with defeat. If it is such, then the "prince of preachers"—a man who lived with great depression *and* great joy in the Lord—must go down in the annals of history as a man of great failure. So too must Jesus Christ be judged for the "heaviness," the excruciating anguish of mind and spirit He suffered by His perfect acquiescence in the will of God. Yet within this total acquiescence in God's will is true joy and strength, even when that will means a Gethsemane (see Matt. 26:36-39).

Joy With Pain
Today we can increase our ability to cope by learn-

ing from Charles Spurgeon that times of depression cannot be eradicated, but that they can be handled constructively.

"The strong are not always vigorous, the wise not always ready, the brave not always courageous, and the joyous not always happy."[2] Such words were not written in the twentieth century by a compromising pastor or psychologist. They were spoken in the nineteenth century by that "Prince of Preachers," Charles Haddon Spurgeon.

In something as common as money, Charles Spurgeon once wrote, "During a very serious illness, I had an unaccountable fit of anxiety about money matters. One of the brethren, after trying to comfort me, went straight home, and came back to me bringing all the stocks and shares and deeds and available funds he had, putting them down on the bed: 'There, dear Pastor, I owe everything I have in the world to you, and you are quite welcome to all I possess.' Of course I soon got better and returned it all to my dear friend."[3] Such was the humanness of Spurgeon, for when it came to money he was often plagued with the kind of anxiety to which many of us can relate.

At the age of 19, he was called to the New Park Street Chapel, one of the leading three (of the 113) Baptist churches of London. He was called because an influential Baptist deacon said, "If you want to fill your empty pews, send for a young man I heard in Cambridge by the name of Spurgeon."[4] Called he was, and the pews filled up until space became an increasing problem.

On October 19, 1856, crowds gathered in a new meeting place which happened to be London's

" 'largest, most commodious and most beautiful building, erected for public amusements, carnivals of wild beasts and wilder men.' It accommodated ten to twelve thousand people. The news of this bold scheme ran through London like wildfire.

". . . the crowd began gathering for the opening service; wild disorder, milling for seats; so that at evening service the hall was packed, and ten thousand more were outside. When Spurgeon saw it he was almost overwhelmed.

"The service began, ran a few minutes, when suddenly a cry, 'Fire! The galleries are giving away, the place is falling!' A terrible panic followed; seven were killed, many seriously injured. Spurgeon's grief over this almost unseated his reason. He was immediately hidden from the public; spent hours 'in tears by day, and dreams of terror by night.' A depression complex deepened upon him from which he never fully recovered.

"But the disaster itself increased the crowds. Charles Haddon Spurgeon became a world figure overnight. On Sunday he was a local celebrity of South London, a 'South of the Slot' hero; the next week he was a world figure. All London now wanted to hear him."[5]

In his lifetime of 57 years Spurgeon published over 3,500 sermons in seventy-five distinct volumes. Writing was drudgery to him; yet he authored 135 books and edited 28 others, totaling more than 200, including albums and pamphlets. This from the man who felt that "writing is the work of a slave!"[6]

"The very last time Spurgeon preached in Metropolitan Tabernacle was the Lord's Day morning of June 7, 1891. He appeared a broken man, 'utterly weary in the Lord's work, but not *of* it'; prematurely old, though but fifty-six; his hair white, anguish lines in his face, so enfeebled that he supported himself with his right hand on the back of a chair. His sermon subject was 'The Statute of David for Sharing the Spoil,' the text 1 Samuel 30:24, 'As his share is that goeth down to the battle, so shall his share be that tarrieth by the baggage; they shall share alike.' Throats were choked in the realization that the end was near. Yet the golden voice, gradually warmed and released by his glowing spirit, filled the Tabernacle with its mellow cadence."[7]

However, "Spurgeon, mighty as he was, could never have moved his generation as he did without the thousands who humbly upheld his hands. None knew this better than he. Once whimsically, he told a story of a French farmer whose crops were so large that he was accused of magic. The man immediately brought forth his stalwart sons and said, 'Here is my magic!' "[8]

Spurgeon did not become great alone. Nor was he a plastic saint. Rather it is his combination of greatness, strength and humanness that has a refreshing appeal to the modern reader. Spurgeon was weak, yet strong. Ill, yet triumphant. He had emotional problems, but they only refined him into the finest of gold which bore the image of that Great Refiner of souls.

For Charles Haddon Spurgeon—the builder of churches, the preacher of preachers, the author of 200 books—could only make us stand in awe. But Charles Haddon Spurgeon—the man who suffered from terrific depression, feared financial disaster, suffered from loneliness, and spent weeks ill in bed—speaks to our present-day needs more deeply than most of our contemporaries.

Says one of his biographers, Richard Day: "There was one aspect of Spurgeon's life, glossed over by most of his biographers, that we must now view with utter frankness: he was frequently in the grip of terrific depression moods. This offers no difficulty whatever to any Christian who does sometimes himself walk the floor of hell, on and on, until he finds a Hand that brings him out. The sweetness of his release giveth him such radiant new love for his Redeemer, that he doth then find in his head the tongue of the taught, enabling him to sustain with words any other that may be weary. The function of 'word sustention' is the chief part of Christian ministry."[9]

Dr. J.H. Jowett who suffered from painful neuritis once said: " 'The world wants to be comforted.' *He* [Spurgeon] *knew that;* and he knew wondrously well how it is done. The tongue of the taught belongs only to those who also are men of sorrows and acquainted with grief."[10]

God's Relief in Depression

In the days of his greatest preaching in the Tabernacle, Spurgeon was often in despair and even thought of quitting, for he felt that his illness too often kept him from the pulpit. Fortunately the leaders of the church felt differently. They preferred Spurgeon with all of his frequent absences to any other man, even one who could be in the pulpit every time the church met. And so Spurgeon stayed. Yet his swollen hands and tired body made him an old man while he was yet young.

"By means of these tragic hours Spurgeon's reliance was kept on God and not on himself. He finally came to the place where he was sure a great blessing was about to break when Depression stormed his soul:

'Depression comes over me whenever the Lord is preparing a larger blessing for my ministry. It has now become to me a prophet in rough clothing. A John the Baptist, heralding the nearer coming of my Lord's richer benison.'

"Often enough he found that richer benison to be a deepened confidence in the sufficiency of grace.... Scarcely had he been pastor of New Park Street 12 months when Asiatic cholera swept like shellfire through the tenement section around the chapel. He gave every ounce of youthful ardor to visiting the sick and dying. But he watched his friends fall one by one, until 'a little more work and weeping would have laid me low among the rest.' Giant Despair had seized him.

"One day, returning from a funeral, ready to sink under the burden, his curiosity led him to read a paper wafered up in a shoemaker's window. In bold handwriting were these words, 'Because thou hast made the Lord, which is my refuge, even the Most High, thy habitation, there shall no evil befall thee, neither shall any plague come nigh thy dwelling.' He said, 'The effect was immediate. I felt secure, refreshed, girt with immortality. I went on with my visitation of the dying in a calm and peaceful spirit.' "[11]

Roots of Depression

Many people I encounter feel that depression is a negative emotion of which they should feel ashamed; and that it comes unbidden out of their own weakness. In contrast, Spurgeon tells of several down-to-earth causes for this unsettling emotion. Because of the painful depression which afflicted him throughout the major part of his life, he took time to analyze the causes.

"The times most favorable to fits of depression, I have experienced, may be summed up in a brief catalogue. First among them I mention *the hour of great success*. When at last a long-cherished desire is fulfilled, when God has been glorified greatly by our means, a great triumph achieved, then we are apt to faint....

"*Before any great achievement,* some measure of the same depression is very usual. Surveying the difficulties before us, our hearts sink within us.... This depression comes over me whenever the Lord is preparing a larger blessing for my ministry....

"*In the midst of a long stretch of unbroken labour,* the same affliction may be looked for. The bow cannot be always bent without fear of breaking. Repose is as needful to the mind as sleep to the body....

"This evil will also come upon us, we know not why, and then it is all the more difficult to drive it away. Causeless depression is not to be reasoned with. . . .If these who laugh at such melancholy did but feel the grief of it for one hour, their laughter would be sobered into compassion."[12]

Without question there can be any number of psychological or physical causes for emotional problems. Help in handling emotional problems is certainly found in a relationship with Jesus Christ, but the complete answer to complex emotional problems may not be spiritual at all. This realization will hopefully save many from feeling guilt over such problems. And recognition of this fact may prevent some from the sin of self-righteously judging others.

Meaning in Pain
Equally important to the cause of depression is its

meaning. Is it a destructive, even sinful emotion? Or is it really a God-allowed instrument of growth and effectiveness?

Frequently in his sermons and in his well-known exposition of the Psalms, Spurgeon spent some pertinent time explaining the meaning of depression. He had found a help in handling his depression: the will to meaning; the importance of having a why for one's existence. Here we have no phony explanation issued from the pen of the unscathed. Rather, we see the pain of one of God's greatest saints made meaningful:

"If it be inquired why the valley of the shadow of death must so often be traversed by the servants of King Jesus, the answer is not far to find. All this is promotive of the Lord's mode of working, which is summed up in these words: 'Not by might nor by power, but by my Spirit, saith the Lord.' Instruments shall be used, but their intrinsic weakness shall be clearly manifested; there shall be no division of the glory, no diminishing the honour due to the Great Worker . . . to hide pride from the worker is the great difficulty. Uninterrupted success and unfading joy in it would be more than our weak heads could bear. Our wine must needs be mixed with water, lest it turn our brains. My witness is, that those who are honored by their Lord in public have usually to endure a secret chastening, or to carry a peculiar cross, lest by any means they exalt themselves, and fall into the snare of the devil. . . .

"By all the castings down of his servants God is glorified, for they are led to magnify him when again he sets them on their feet, and even while prostrate in the dust their faith yields him praise. They speak all the more sweetly of his faithfulness, and are the more firmly established in his love. . . . Glory be to God for the furnace, the hammer, and the fire. Heaven shall be all the fuller of bliss because we have been filled with anguish here below, and earth shall be better tilled because of our training in the school of adversity."[13]

God never wastes His children's suffering. I repeatedly have seen persons who can bear their burdens no longer, released from the mental anguish of depression and restored to normal life at just that "right moment" in God's timetable.

Spurgeon also affirms this principle:

"To the tearful eye of the sufferer the Lord seemed to stand still, as if he calmly looked on, and did not sympathize with his afflicted one. Nay, more, the Lord appeared to be afar off, no longer 'a very present help in trouble,' but an inaccessible mountain, into which no man would be able to climb. The presence of God is the joy of his people but any suspicion of his absence is distracting beyond measure. Let us, then, remember that the Lord is nigh us. The refiner is never far from the mouth of the furnace when the gold is in that fire, and the Son of God is always walking in the midst of the flames when his holy children are cast into them. Yet he knows that the frailty of man will little wonder that when we are sharply exercised, we find it hard to bear the apparent neglect of the Lord when he forbears to work our deliverance. . . . It is not the trouble, but the hiding of our Father's face, which cuts us to the quick. . . . If we need an answer to the question, 'Why hidest thou thyself?' it is to be found in the fact that there is a 'needs-be,' not only for trial, but for heaviness of heart under trial (1 Peter 1:6)—for it is only *felt* affliction which can become *blest* affliction. If we are carried in the arms of God over every stream, where would be the trial and where the experience, which trouble is meant to teach us?"[14]

This concept is antithetical to certain present-day teaching which presents depression and pain as sin and as indications of God's disciplining.

Discipline in Suffering

Spurgeon sheds further positive light on the significance of suffering for those beset by great trials:

"The Lord frequently appears to save his heaviest blows for his best-loved ones; if any one affliction be more painful than another it falls to the lot of those whom he most distinguishes in his service. The gardener prunes his best roses with most care. [Discipline] is sent to keep successful saints humble, to make them tender towards others, and to enable them to bear the high honours which their heavenly Friend puts upon them. 'But he hath not given me over unto death.' This verse . . . concludes with a blessed 'but,' which constitutes a saving clause. . . . There is always a merciful limit to the [disciplining] of the sons of God. Forty stripes save one were all that an Israelite might receive, and the Lord will never allow that one, that killing stroke, to fall upon his children. They are '[disciplined], but not killed.'

"Even from our griefs we may distill consolation and gather sweet flowers from the garden in which the Lord has planted salutary rue and wormwood . . . The hero, restored to health, and rescued from the dangers of battle, now lifts up his own song unto the Lord, and asks all Israel, led on by the goodly fellowship of priests, to assist him in chanting a joyful Te Deum."[15]

Exchanging the word "heaviness" for the word "depression," Spurgeon continues his thoughts on its meaning:

"If the Christian did not sometimes suffer heaviness he would begin to grow too proud, and think too much of himself, and become too great in his own esteem. Those of us who are of elastic spirit, and who in our health are full of everything that can make life happy, are too apt to forget that all our own springs must be in him . . ."

"Another reason for this discipline is, I think, that in heaviness we often learn lessons that we never could attain elsewhere. Do you know that God has beauties for every part of the world; and he has beauties for every place of experience? There are views to be seen from the tops of the Alps that you can never see elsewhere. Ay, but there are beauties to be seen in the depths of the dell that ye could never see on the tops of the mountains; there are glories to be seen on Pisgah, wondrous sights to be beheld when by faith we stand on Tabor; but there are also beauties to be seen in our Gethsemanes, and some marvellously sweet flowers to be called by the edge of the dens of the leopards. Men will never become great in divinity until they become great in suffering. "Ah!" said Luther, "affliction is the best book in my library,' and let me add, the best leaf in the book of affliction is that blackest of all the leaves, the leaf called heaviness, when the spirit sinks within us, and we cannot endure as we could wish.

"And yet again; this heaviness is of essential use to a Christian, if he would do good to others. Ah! There are a great many Christian people that I was going to say I should like to see afflicted—but I will not say so much as that; I should like to see them heavy in spirit; if it were the Lord's will that they should be bowed down greatly, I would not express a word of reget; for a little more . . . power to sympathize would be a precious boon to them, and even if it were purchased by a short journey through a burning, fiery furnace, they might not rue the day afterwards in which they had been called to pass through the flame. There are none so tender as those who have been skinned themselves. Those who have been in the chamber of affliction know how to comfort those who are there. Do not believe that any man will become a physician unless he walks the hospitals; and I am sure that no one will become a divine, or become a comforter, unless he lies in the hospital as well as walks through it and has to suffer himself. God cannot make ministers—and I speak with reverence of His Holy Name—he cannot make a Barnabas except in the fire. It is there, and there alone, that he can make his sons of consolation; he may make his sons of thunder anywhere; but his sons of consolation he must make in the fire, and there alone. Who shall speak to those whose hearts are broken, who shall bind up their wounds, but those whose hearts have been broken also, and whose wounds have long run with the sore of grief? 'If need be,' then, 'ye are in heaviness through manifold temptation.' "16

Growth Through Distress

How easily we equate happiness with success and well-being. Even as Christians we often deceive ourselves into believing that we are obligated to achieve perpetual happiness. The Bible does not teach such a principle; rather it promises a deep spiritual contentment even in the depth of suffering. Charles Spurgeon knew above and beyond any mere psychological implication that spiritual growth and greatness are often mixed with pain; in his case, the pain of periodic and intense depression.

"Our work, when earnestly undertaken, lays us open to attacks in the direction of depression. Who can bear the weight of souls without sinking to the dust? Passionate longings after men's conversion, if not fully satisfied (and when are they?), consume the soul with anxiety and disappointment. To see the hopeful turn aside, the godly grow cold, professors abusing their privileges, and sinners waxing more bold in sin—are not these sights enough to crush us to the earth? . . . How can we be otherwise than sorrowful while men believe not our report, and the divine arm is not revealed? All mental work tends to weary and to depress, for much study is a weariness of the flesh; but ours is more than mental work—it is heart work, the labour of our inmost soul . . . Such soul-travail as that of a faithful minister will bring on occasional seasons of exhaustion, when heart and flesh will fail. Moses' hands grew heavy in intercession, and Paul cried out, "Who is sufficient for these things?" Even John the Baptist is thought to have had his fainting fits, and the apostles were once amazed, and were sore afraid."[17]

As he stated earlier when giving the causes for depression, Spurgeon perceived an unnecessary form of depression arising from too much study and too little exercise. As the author of more than 200 works and preacher of hundreds of sermons, such depression was a continuing problem for Spurgeon: "I confess that I frequently sit hour after hour praying and waiting for a subject, and that is the main part of my study. Almost every Sunday of my life I prepare enough outlines of sermons to last me for a month."[18]

For Charles Haddon Spurgeon, the most solemn place in the world was the pulpit. And he went into it week after week, obviously depending upon the Holy Spirit. Such mental and spiritual intensity took its toll.

There can be little doubt that sedentary habits have a tendency to create despondency in some constitutions. "Burton, in his *Anatomy of Melancholy,* has a chapter upon this cause of sadness; and quoting from one of the myriad authors whom he lays under contribution, he says: 'Students are negligent of their bodies. Other men look to their tools: a painter will wash his pencils; a smith will look to his hammer, anvil, forge; a husbandman will mend his plough-irons, and grind his hatchet if it be dull; a falconer or huntsman will have an especial care of his hawks, hounds, horses, dogs, etc.; a musician will string and unstring his lute; only scholars neglect that instrument (their brain and spirits, I mean) which they daily use.'

"To sit long in one posture, poring over a book, or driving a quill, is in itself a taxing of nature; but add to this a badly ventilated chamber, a body which has long been without muscular exercise, and a heart burdened with many cares, and we have all the elements for preparing a seething cauldron of despair, especially in the dim months of fog—

"When a blanket wraps the day,
   When the rotten woodland drips,
   And the leaf is stamped in clay.
Let a man be naturally as blithe as a bird, he will hardly

be able to bear up year after year against such a suicidal process; he will make his study a prison and his books the warders of a gaol, while nature lies outside his window calling him to health and beckoning him to joy. He who forgets the humming of the bees among the heather, the cooing of the wood pigeons in the forest, the song of birds in the woods, the rippling of rills among the rushes, and the sighing of the wind among the pines, need not wonder if his heart forgets to sing and his soul grows heavy. A day's breathing of fresh air upon the hills, or a few hours' ramble in the beechwood's umbrageous calm, would sweep the cobwebs out of the brain of scores of our toiling ministers who are now but half alive. A mouthful of sea air, or a stiff walk in the wind's face, would not give grace to the soul, but it would yield oxygen to the body, which is the next best.

"Heaviest the heart is in a heavy air,
  Ev'ry wind that rises blows away despair.

" 'The ferns and the rabbits, the streams and the trout, the fir trees and the squirrels, the primroses and the violets, the farmyard, the new-mown hay, and the fragrant hops—these are the best medicines for hypochondriacs, the surest tonics for the declining, the best refreshments for the weary.' For lack of opportunity, or inclination, these great remedies are neglected, and the student becomes a self-immolated victim."[19]

Much of our fatigue and depression is the result of refusal to take small breaks and short vacations. One weekend recently I escaped from the demands of patients to my favorite ocean cottage which has no telephones. I walked on the wet sand and thought about God's timelessness as I watched the waves crash against the rocks. By Monday I was refreshed and ready to go back to work because I had taken time away. Never should we underestimate the value of even small breaks.

Ahead of his time, Spurgeon was sensitive to the needs of the body as it related to the needs of the mind. He had discovered the value of rest and recreation in averting and ameliorating depression.

Referring to Jesus' response to His weary disciples—"Let us go into the desert and rest awhile" (Mark 6:31)—Spurgeon comments: "What? When the people are fainting? When they are like sheep without a shepherd? How can Jesus talk of rest? When the scribes and Pharisees, like wolves, are rending the flock, how can he take his followers on an excursion into a quiet resting place? . . . The Lord Jesus knows better. He will not exhaust the strength of his servants prematurely and quench the light of Israel. Rest time is not waste. It is economy to gather fresh strength. Look at the mower in the summer's day, with so much to cut down ere the sun sets. He pauses in his labour—is he a sluggard? He looks for his stone, and begins to draw it up and down his scythe, with *rink-a-tink, rink-a-tink.* Is that idle music—is he wasting precious moments? How much might he have mowed while he has been ringing out those notes on his scythe! But he is sharpening his tool, and he will do far more when once again he gives his strength to those sweeps which lay the grass prostrate in rows before him. Nor can the fisherman be always fishing; he must mend his nets. So even our vacation can be one of the duties laid upon us by the kingdom of God."[20]

In our work-oriented society, some of us are geared to feeling a sense of guilt regarding rest and recreation. Though we appear to place a premium on leisure time, many of us are prone to combining vacations with business trips or spending days off worrying about business or financial problems. In light of this, Spurgeon's point is profoundly significant: a vacation is a *duty God* requires of us!

Flawed Vessels

It is impossible to speak of depression as a problem arising only from one source. As each of us is a composite of body, mind and soul, problems in any of these areas of our personhood can cause depression. I sometimes deal with patients who have emotional problems arising from physical causes. These patients sometimes have difficulty believing that their emotional negativism and hopelessness can be the result of physical malfunctions.

Spurgeon was far ahead of his time in perceiving this important relationship between emotions and the body. Perhaps this was due in part to his own deep suffering labeled as gout, which is now known to be a painful form of arthritis arising from an overabundance of uric acid in the system. In his physical weakness and pain he often slumped into the depths of despair. For that reason Spurgeon knew better than most people today the relationship between his emotions and his body:

"*Most of us are in some way or other unsound physically.* 'Here and there we meet with an old man who could not remember that ever he was laid aside for a day; but the great mass of us labour under some form or other of infirmity, either in body or mind. . . . As to mental maladies, is any man altogether sane? Are we not all a little off the balance? Some minds appear to have a gloomy tinge essential to their very individuality;

of them it may be said, "Melancholy marked them for her own"—fine minds withal, and ruled by noblest principles, but yet most prone to forget the silver lining, and to remember only the cloud. . . . These infirmities may be no detriment to a man's career of special usefulness; they may even have been imposed upon him by divine wisdom as necessary qualifications for his peculiar course of service. Some plants owe their medicinal qualities to the marsh in which they grow; others to the shades in which alone they flourish. There are precious fruits put forth by the moon as well as by the sun. Boats need ballast as well as sail; a drag on the carriage wheel is no hindrance when the road runs downhill. Pain has, probably, in some cases developed genius, hunting out the soul which otherwise might have slept like a lion in its den. Had it not been for the broken wing, some might have lost themselves in the clouds, some even of these choice doves who now bear the olive branch in their mouths and show the way to the ark. But where in body and mind there are predisposing causes to lowness of spirit, it is no marvel if in dark moments the heart succumbs to them; the wonder in many cases is—and if inner lives could be written, men would see it so—how some . . . keep at their work at all, and still wear a smile upon their countenances. . . . 'Blessed are they that mourn,' said the Man of Sorrows, and let none account themselves otherwise when their tears are salted with grace. We have the treasure of the gospel in earthen vessels, and if there be a flaw in the vessel here and there, let none wonder.' "[21]

Compassion from Suffering

Many patients tell how they have been able to help

others. Sometimes the very best antidote for depression is the understanding another person can offer. Spurgeon through his own pain discusses compassion as an outgrowth of depression.

"How low the spirits of good and brave men will sometimes sink. Under the influence of certain disorders everything will wear a sombre aspect, and the heart will dive into the profoundest days of misery. It is all very very well for those who are in robust health and full of spirits to blame those whose lives are [covered over] with melancholy, but the [pain] is as real as a gaping wound, and all the more hard to bear because it lies as much in the region of the soul that to the inexperienced it appears to be a mere matter of fancy and imagination. Reader, never ridicule the nervous and hypochondriacal, their pain is real—it is not imaginary. . . . The mind can descend far lower than the body . . . flesh can bear only a certain number of wounds and no more, but the soul can bleed in ten thousand ways and die over and over again each hour. It is grievous to the good man to see the Lord whom he loves laying him in the sepulchre of desponding . . . yet if faith could but be allowed to speak she would remind the depressed saint that it is better to fall into the hand of the Lord than into the hands of men, and moreover she would tell the despondent heart that God never placed Joseph in a pit without drawing him up again to fill a throne . . . . Alas, when under deep depression the mind forgets all this and is only conscious of its unutterable misery. . . . It is an unspeakable consolation that our Lord Jesus knows this experience, right well, having with the exception of the sin of it, felt it all and more than all in Gethsemane when he was exceedingly sorrowful even unto death."[22]

By sharing his pain, Spurgeon was able to help others. Even in the pulpit, to a large congregation he once said: "I would go into the deeps a hundred times to cheer a downcast spirit. It is good for me to have been afflicted, that I might know how to speak a word in season to one that is weary."[23]

That such was true in Spurgeon's life was shown in a letter he received after a severe down period: "Here is a specimen showing how Spurgeon was able to comfort others with the same comfort whereby he was comforted. From Montreal came this rewarding letter.

" 'Oh, Mr. Spurgeon, that little word of yours, "I am feeling low," struck a chord which still vibrates in my spirit. It was to me like reading the Forty-second Psalm. I imagine there is nothing in your ministry to the saints that comes home more tenderly to tried and stricken souls than just what you there express, "I am feeling low." The great preacher, the author of *The Treasury of David*, this man sometimes, aye, often, "feels low" just as they do. In all their affliction he was afflicted—this is what draws hearts to Jesus; and the principle is just the same when the friends and intimates of Jesus "feel low." The fellow feeling, thus begotten, makes many wondrous kind.

Your friend in Jesus,
John Louson.' "[24]

Christians may find themselves vulnerable to criticism from Christians and non-Christians alike when they are suffering times of depression. Charles Spurgeon was certainly no exception. He was often criticized for his vulnerability to depression. But without the compassion Spurgeon demonstrated in his own affliction, countless others suffering like him would not have been comforted.

Praying to Cope

Rather than withering under the pressure of depression or groveling in guilt over his supposed weakness or sin, Spurgeon proclaims the relationship of anguish and prayer; "When our prayers are lowly . . . by reason of our despondency," Spurgeon wrote, "the Lord will bow down to them, the infinitely exalted Jehovah will have respect unto them. Faith, when she has the loftiest name of God on her tongue . . . dares to ask from him the most tender and condescending acts of love. Great as he is he loves his children to be bold with him. Our distress is a forcible reason for our being heard by the Lord God, merciful, and gracious, for misery is ever the master argument with mercy."[25]

God never fails to hear our prayers. Indeed, the God who "numbers the hairs on our heads" and "preserves our tears in bottles" cannot fail to be concerned with our pain.

Again Spurgeon emphasizes the importance of prayer as a weapon against depression in his famous work written about the Psalms. Quoting from Psalm 102:23,24—"He weakened my strength in the way; he shortened my days. I said, O my God, take me not away in the midst of my days"—Spurgeon says, in relationship to the psalmist's feelings and ultimate prayer: the psalmist "pours out his personal complaint. His sorrow had cast down his spirit, and even caused weakness in his bodily frame—and [he] was ready to lie down and die . . . He [gave] himself to prayer: What better remedy is there for depression? Good men should not dread death, but they are not forbidden to love life: for many reasons the man who has the best hope of heaven, may nevertheless think it desirable to continue here a little longer, for the sake of his family, his work, the church of God and even the glory of God itself. [They say,] do not swirl me away like Elijah in a chariot of fire, for as yet I have only seen half my days, and that a sorrowful half; give me to live till the flustering morning shall have softened into a bright afternoon of happier existence."[26]

We Shall Be Like Him

Too often we forget that Jesus Christ is God who became man and was subject to all the emotions that normal men feel. In a sermon preached at the Music Hall in Royal Surrey Gardens on November 7, 1858, Spurgeon drew upon the reality of Jesus the man, and uniquely presented depression as "being in heaviness" as our Lord was at times in His earthly life:

"It is a rule of the kingdom that all members must be like the head. They are to be like the head in that day when he shall appear. 'We shall be like him, for we shall see him as he is.' But we must be like the head also in his humiliation, or else we cannot be like him in his glory. Now you will observe that our Lord and Saviour Jesus Christ very often passed through much of trouble, without any heaviness. When he said, 'Foxes have holes, and the birds of the air have nests, but the Son of Man hath not where to lay his head,' I observe no heaviness. I do not think he sighed over that. And when athirst he sat upon the well, and said, 'Give me to drink,' there was no heaviness in all his thirst. I believe that through the first years of his ministry, although he might have suffered some heaviness, he usually passed over his troubles like a ship floating over the waves of the sea. But you will remember that at last the waves of swelling grief came into the vessel; at last the Saviour himself, though full of patience, was obliged to say 'My soul is exceeding sorrowful, even unto death'; and one of the evangelists tells us that the Saviour 'began to be very heavy.' What means that, but that his spirits began to sink? There is more terrible meaning yet . . . the surface meaning of it is that all his spirits sank with him. He had no longer his wonted courage, and though he had strength to say, 'Nevertheless, not my will, but thine be done,' still the weakness did not prevail, when he said, 'If it be possible let this cup pass from me,' The Saviour passed through the brook, but he 'drank of the brook by the way'; and we who pass through the brook of suffering must drink of it too. He had to bear the burden, not with his shoulders omnipotent, but with shoulders that were bending to the earth beneath a load. And you and I must not always expect a giant faith that can remove mountains: sometimes even to us the grasshopper must be a burden, that we may in all things be like our head."[27]

Yet the black clouds of depression never permanently left Spurgeon's life until he entered into life with his Saviour. Through all those earthly days, God was enough, "the true source of all consolation."

Referring to Psalms 102:3 where the psalmist says, "For my days are consumed like smoke," Spurgeon comments: "My grief has made life unsubstantial to me, I seem to be but a puff, a vapour which has nothing in it, and is soon dissipated. The metaphor is very admirably chosen, for, to the unhappy, life seems not merely to be frail, but to be surrounded by so much that is darkening, defiling, blinding, and depressing, that, sitting down in despair, they compare themselves to men wandering in a dense fog. . . ." Spurgeon continues: "Now the writer's mind is turned away from his personal and relative troubles to the true source of all consolation, namely, the Lord himself, and his gracious purposes toward His own people. 'But thou, O Lord, shalt endure forever.' I perish, but thou wilt not."[28]

The Light Beyond

In spite of and very likely because of the depression in Spurgeon's life, he became a spiritual giant for God. Biographer Richard Day confesses that "he was unexpectedly moved to tears in reading one of Spurgeon's travelog lectures." Within seven lines of the end, Spurgeon suddenly concluded his remarks: "If you cannot travel, remember that our Lord Jesus Christ is more glorious than all else that you could ever see. Get a view of Christ and you have seen more than mountains and cascades and valleys and seas can ever show you. Earth may give its beauty, and stars their brightness, but all these put together can never rival Him."[29]

"Tirshatha"—as Susannah Spurgeon called her husband, using the Hebrew word for the Reverence— spent some of his winter months in Mentone, France, because his body could not endure the chill of London. Susannah, who became an invalid at the age of 33, was unable to travel and go with him. During one of those winter separations, Spurgeon wrote this to his wife: "You are the precise form in which God would make a woman for such a man as I." Such a woman she truly was. "Many times Spurgeon came home from meetings at the great tabernacle exhausted and in the grip of depression. Then she would read to him from Baxter's *Reformed Pastor*—"he would weep at my feet, and I would weep too.'"[30]

Susannah herself knew the purposes of suffering.

Watching a crackling oak log on the fireplace one evening, she wrote: "We are like this old log. We should give forth no melodious sounds were it not for the fire."[31]

In God's gracious plan, Susannah Spurgeon was strong enough to go to France with her husband the year of his death. "When he lay dying in Mentone, Susannah lingered beside him. She wept softly as he lay for hours unconscious. She smiled bravely through her tears when for short intervals he spoke with her. Out of her grief she wrote: 'Perhaps of greatest price among the precious things which this little book (the *Secret Diary*) reveals, is the beloved author's personal and intense love for the Lord Jesus. He lived in His embrace; like the apostle John, his head leaned on Jesu's bosom ('Jesu' was his private and intimate term of endearment for his Lord). The endearing terms, used in the Diary and never discontinued, were not empty words.'

"When the end drew near, he whispered, 'Susie.' She bent close to listen, clasped his hand in hers and said, 'Yes, dear Tirshatha.' And he murmured—the last words before he saw Him face to face—'Oh, wifie, I have had such a blessed time with my Lord.' "[32]

"Years before [Spurgeon] had spoken of death: 'The dying saint is not in a flurry; he keeps to his old pace—he walks. The last days of a Christian are the most peaceful of his whole career; many a saint has reaped more joy and knowledge when he came to die than ever he knew while he lived. When there is a shadow, there must be a light somewhere. The light of Jesus shining upon death throws a shadow across our path; let us therefore rejoice for the Light beyond!' "[33]

Notes

All material quoted is used by permission.

1. Amy Carmichael, *Gold Cord* (Fort Washington, PA: Christian Literature Crusade, Inc., 1957), p. 268.

2. Helmut Thielicke, John W. Doberstein, trans., *Encounter with Spurgeon* (Grand Rapids: Baker Book House, 1975), p. 214. © 1963 by Fortress Press.

3. Richard E. Day, *The Shadow of the Broad Brim* (Philadelphia: Judson Press, 1934), p. 175.

4. Ibid., p. 85.

5. Ibid., p. 96.

6. Ibid., p. 185.

7. Ibid., p. 197.

8. Ibid., p. 198.

9. Ibid., p. 173.

10. Ibid.

11. Ibid., pp. 177,178.

12. Thielicke, op. cit., pp. 218-222.

13. Ibid., pp. 222,223.

14. Charles H. Spurgeon, *The Treasury of David* (Grand Rapids: Zondervan Publishing House, 1966), vol. 1, p. 110.

15. Ibid., vol. 3., p. 108.

16. Charles H. Spurgeon, *New Park Street Pulpit 1858* (London: Banner of Truth Trust, 1964), vol. 4, pp. 400-461.

17. Thielicke, op. cit., p. 216.

18. Ernest W. Bacon, *Spurgeon: Heir of the Puritans* (Grand Rapids: William B. Eerdmans Publishing Co., 1968), p. 78.

19. Thielicke, op. cit., pp. 217,218.

20. Ibid., p. 11.

21. Ibid., p. 215.

22. Spurgeon, *Treasury*, vol. 2., pp. 3,4.

23. Day, op. cit., p. 178.

24. Ibid., p. 179.

25. Spurgeon, op. cit., vol. 2, p. 463.

26. Ibid., pp. 254,257.

27. Spurgeon, *New Park Street*, p. 460.

28. Spurgeon, op. cit., pp. 251,254.

29. Day, op. cit., p. 226.

30. Ibid., p. 113.

31. Ibid., p. 115.

32. Ibid., p. 227.

33. Bacon, op. cit., p. 167.

CHAPTER 3

Coping with Suffering

An Insight into the Life of Amy Carmichael

On a dull Sunday morning in Belfast, a young girl walked home from a fashionable church and encountered a pathetic old woman carrying a heavy bundle. Impulsively the girl helped her. Then, with horror, she thought that "respectable" people might see her. It was a moment of decision. Then in her mind flashed the words: "Gold, silver, precious stones, wood, hay, stubble. . . . If any man's work abide . . ." (1 Cor. 3:12,14). She looked around her and everything seemed normal. But, said Amy Carmichael later, "I knew that something had happened that had changed life's values. Nothing could ever matter again but the things that were eternal."

Only That Which Is Eternal

Woven throughout her writings, "nothing is important but that which is eternal," remains a theme carried out in practical terms with family relationships, friendships, or something as deep as illness and death. It is a principle which casts a new and vital perspective on how each of us lives.

In a fast changing society with our fluctuating values we find it difficult to even know what it means to live under God's approval. "God can't love me. I'm no good," said one lady sadly as she sat down in my office. Another young woman refused psychological help because she "can get all she needs from reading the Bible."

A young man brought his child to see me at the advice of his pastor; then he admitted that his real reason for coming was to talk about his extramarital affair—an affair of which the pastor had no knowledge and which, apart from being discovered, did not on the surface disturb the young man. When I asked him how he reconciled his sexual activity with his biblical knowledge, he replied, "I don't try to."

In the midst of such obvious confusion in a society which changes so fast that Christians too lose a perspective as to what God wants, Amy Carmichael offers an old but continuingly current point of view. Like the rest of us, she struggled to learn what God wanted of her. From that early moment in Belfast to the last years of total invalidism she fought to know God's approval, and in the process gives us a believable example of coping with suffering.

A physical breakdown when she was a missionary in Japan merely sent her to a life in southern India, rescuing children sold to the gods as temple prostitutes. There she actually took on Indian citizenship and melted into the Indian culture. Yet her goal was to do her work as Christ had done His on this earth.

In 1919, when she was awarded a high honor and was presented with a medal from the governor of Madras, she almost refused it. "It troubles me," she said, "to have an experience so different from His Who was despised and rejected—not kindly honored."[1]

Miss Carmichael's standards were high. She insisted upon the children being raised with the highest standards of honesty and loyalty. That the Dohnavur Fellowship of India still exists is evidence that her standards were not so high, however, as to be spiritually unrealistic. That she could be very practical was evidenced when she traveled long journeys on hot dusty roads to rescue an ill child. At the root of all her endeavors and in the midst of all her suffering was the deep desire to live under God's approval in all circumstances. Perhaps her attitude toward life can be summarized in one of her poems, "Make Me Thy Fuel":

From prayer that asks that I may be
Sheltered from winds that beat on Thee,
From fearing when I should aspire,
From faltering when I should climb higher.
From silken self, O Captain, free
Thy soldier who would follow Thee.

From subtle love of softening things,
From easy choices, weakenings,
Not thus are spirits fortified,
Not this way went the Crucified,
From all that dims Thy Calvary,
O Lamb of God, deliver me.

Give me the love that leads the way,
The faith that nothing can dismay,
The hope no disappointments tire,
The passion that will burn like fire,
Let me not sink to be a clod;
Make me Thy fuel, Flame of God.[2]

The problem of God's approval becomes even more complicated when suffering is involved. Perhaps one of the toughest issues that a thinking person faces— and certainly a psychotherapist who daily witnesses the inner torture of so many—is the problem of pain. Nietzsche has quite accurately stated that "He who knows the *why* to his existence can endure *any how.*"

Sometimes the *how* hurts so badly that the *why* is hard to remember. It is hard for a small child to work for eight years to walk. The *how* seems too tedious and painful; the *why* feels remote and at times seemingly unattainable. And sometimes the *why* becomes obscure or is unknowable to finite minds. Why do people starve to death or nearly starve? Why do little children at age three need therapy for emotional problems so deeply engrained that scars remain for life? Why, on a human level, does life seem so much more filled with pain than pleasure, with mere survival as a primary goal for many?

Amy Carmichael comments in her various books on different aspects of human suffering which affects us all. In so doing she casts a meaning and a purpose on even the severest difficulties of life which is strengthening as well as enlightening.

Frequently, Christians who try to live in the light of eternity have severe doubts about their ability to do so. We know that we should love, but we find it difficult to love the unlovable. We fear failure and criticism, especially when we suffer and are criticized. Amy Carmichael describes this well when she writes: "Some are wonderfully created. They can go through a thick flight of stinging arrows and hardly feel them. It is as if they were clad in fine chain-armour.

"Others are made differently. The arrows pierce, and most sharply if they be shot by friends. The very tone of a voice can depress such a one for a week. (It can uplift, too; for the heart that is open to hurt is also very open to love.)

"The Indian [referring to the native of India] has by nature no chain-armour, and some of us can understand just what that means. But if we are to be God's knights, we must learn to go through flights of arrows, and so the teaching which was set on fashioning warriors, not weaklings, often dealt with this."[3] Again, Miss Carmichael's emphasis here is not on the eradication of suffering, but on the Christian's coping with it.

Coping with Being Misunderstood

The principle upon which Amy Carmichael operated under criticism is reflected in two of her illustrations: "Walker of Tinnevelly sat alone in his study reading the copy of a document addressed to the Archbishop of Canterbury. It was a petition against him and one or two other true men who had stood by him in his efforts to cut certain cankers out of this South Indian Church. It was an amazing composition, cruel and false because so ignorant.

"[Walker] came out from his study that day looking very white, and his eyes were like dark fires. But he went straight on like a man walking through cobwebs stretched across his path. And what does it matter now? He has seen his Lord's face. *All that troubles is only for a moment. Nothing is important but that which is eternal.*"[4]

In another instance Miss Carmichael spoke of her own experience in a setting where alcohol was forbidden to a "good Christian" and she was misrepresented in her presentation of the subject: "One of the first meetings she was asked to take in India was for English soldiers belonging to a South Indian cantonment. It was supposed to be a Temperance meeting, but Temperance was hardly mentioned. The soldiers needed something that went much deeper. That meeting was reported in the Parish magazine. An address had been given on the benefits of alcohol. It had come as a pleasant surprise, the writer said, to hear from a missionary that alcohol was beneficial.

"For a minute a quite young missionary felt this rather staggering. And then suddenly the thought came, 'It won't matter fifty years hence, so what does it matter now?' Nothing is important but that which is eternal."[5] So often it was the principle of viewing life in an eternal perspective which enabled Amy Carmichael to cope with suffering.

In my work as a counselor I see many who feel hurt from unjust criticism for the idleness and, indeed, savagery of words can be felt as a very deep form of suffering. But perhaps those who feel the most criticism at times are those who are in positions of power, particularly in Christian work. A leader in the Christian world is troubled by a disturbed child. Instead of being upheld he is often criticized by fellow Christians. Illness is regarded as lack of faith in some circles. Men earnestly helping with the emotional problems of their congregation find themselves suddenly accused of a sexual affair. For such the words, "nothing matters but that which is eternal" is at times the only effective antidote.

Coping with Physical Illness

In speaking of another form of suffering—chronic physical pain—Amy Carmichael recounts this instance: "One of our Indian Viceroys, perhaps the most dazzling figure of them all, could not stand to face an audience without the support of a steel device. 'I, at times, suffer terribly from my back,' he wrote from out of the blaze of public life, 'and one day it will finish me. But so long as one is marching, I say, let the drums beat and the flags by.' (Not many knew of that gnawing pain. Perhaps if it were remembered that often there is sackcloth under royal robes, the judgment of the world would be kinder.)

"Whatever the Iron Crown may be, so long as one is marching let the drums beat and the flags by. What does it matter that no one knows the cost of those brave words? He whose crown was of thorns knows all that is covered from casual glance of man. Where others see merely a decorous exterior, He sees a soul, sometimes a tortured soul, looking up into His eyes for courage and grace to live triumphantly a moment at a time. And if we could hear spiritual voices speak, we should hear something like this, 'Thy flesh and thy heart faileth? I know, my child, I know. But I am the strength of thy heart and thy portion for ever. Thou shalt not be forgotten of Me.' "[6]

Those who are well are sometimes not able to understand and accept those who are ill. As one patient said to me, "If my friend is sick I'm sorry; but she's going to have to forget it and go back to work. After all, her rent has to be paid." Or worse still is the comment directed to the young girl who was told that she was in braces only because she didn't have enough faith.

Miss Carmichael shows profound sensitivity when she writes: "There are some for whom illness is made more difficult than it need be. Boswell shivers on the chilly boat-journey from Greenwich to London, 'for the night air was so cold that it made me shiver. I was the more sensible of it from having sat up all the night before, recollecting and writing in my journal what I thought worthy of preservation' (of the sayings and doings of his friend). But Johnson, who 'was not in the least affected by the cold, scolded me as if my shivering had been a paltry effeminacy.' Another unfortunate is rebuked for a headache: 'At your age, Sir, I had no head-ache.' There is one simple way to achieve serenity when (if ever) we meet Dr. Samuel Johnson: It is to be glad that he had never known 'shivering' or 'head-ache.' And also to remember that he is probably like a Spanish chestnut, rather pickly outside, but inside very good."[7]

In commenting on the health of a fellow Indian nurse, Kohila, Amy Carmichael says intuitively: "But, 'God help us if we are not better than our bodies' inclinations'; the spirit of man will sustain his infirmity, is a great word for the ill, if only by the grace of the Lord, the Conqueror of pain, they can lay hold upon it. And Kohila did. Her fellow-nurses say of her, 'She was not an ordinary patient. She never forgot that she was a nurse, and so must be a perfect patient.' From time to time also there were the trials and tests that must be if life is to be more than a painted pretence. Each one of these had a share in shaping the child of this story. We thought of everything as a preparation for service, witness-bearing and soul-winning in the Place of Healing and in the villages. But now we know that it was preparation for another Service, Elsewhere."[8]

Joy Is Coping

Perhaps some of Amy Carmichael's best words on illness, however, come from her book, *Rose from Brier,* where she writes, "from the ill to the ill." Sensitive to a lack of understanding from those who are well, she writes from her own illness:

"One day, after weeks of nights when, in spite of all that was done to induce sleep, it refused to come, except in brief distracted snatches, the mail brought a letter which discoursed with what sounded almost like plea-sure on this 'enforced rest,' and the silly phrase rankled like a thorn. I was far too tired to laugh it off as one can laugh off things when one is well. So *this* was supposed to be rest? And was the Father breaking, crushing, 'forcing,' by weight of sheer physical misery, a child who only longed to obey His lightest wish? This word had what I now know was an absurd power to distress. It held such an unkind, such a false conception of our Father. Till that hour, although I was puzzled, I had not had one unhappy minute. I had been given peace in acceptance. The spirit can live above the flesh, and mine, helped by the tender love of our Lord Jesus and the dearness of all around me, had done so.

"But in that hour it was different, and I had no peace till I had heard deep within me soft and soothing words such as a mother uses: 'Let not your heart be troubled; do I not understand? What do such words matter to Me or to thee?" And I knew that the Father understood His child, and the child her Father, and all was peace again."[9]

Approval from God is sometimes most intensely enjoyed when the suffering and the abrasiveness are hidden from man and known only to God. For we are quick to laud those whom we can *see* as brave. A man with a cane or a child in braces is praised for bravery, and should be. But the person with depressive feelings or the person quietly suffering from the news of terminal illness in the life of a loved one is told to "rejoice" or "cheer up." The result in the sufferer is discouragement and, at times, is a feeling that not even God understands.

In an era of "Praise the Lord" theology, the real meaning of words like praise and joy may become lost to superficiality. For it is only in deep suffering that people know the depths of all emotion, whether it be pain that is almost unbearable even for one moment more, or joy that sweeps over the soul once that pain is gone. On an even more profound level, joy can exist *with* pain if one accurately defines that joy.

"Thunder-clouds are nothing to the Spirit of Joy. The only special reference to the joy of the Holy Spirit is bound up with the words 'much affliction,' much pressure. It is the rose under thunder-cloud again." Miss Carmichael includes the words of Webb-Peploe as she continues.

" 'Joy is not gush; joy is not jolliness. Joy is simply perfect acquiescence in God's will, because the soul delights itself in God Himself. Christ took God as His God and Father, and that brought Him at last to say, "I delight to do Thy will," though the cup was the cross, in such agony as no man knew. It cost Him blood. *It cost Him blood.* O take the Fatherhood of God in the blessed Son the Saviour, and by the Holy Ghost rejoice, rejoice in the will of God, and in nothing else. Bow down your heads and your hearts before God, and let the will, the blessed will of God, be done.'

"These weighty words were spoken by Prebendary Webb-Peploe to a gathering of Christians many years ago. In the silence that closed the hour, the speaker—some knew it—was laying, not for the first time, his Isaac on the altar of his God. It is the life lived that gives force to the words spoken. These words were not wind and froth. They sound through the years like the deep notes of a bell: *'Joy is not gush; joy is not jolliness. Joy is perfect acquiescence in the will of God.'*

"This, then, is the call to the climbing soul. Expose yourself to the circumstances of His choice, for that is perfect acquiescence in the will of God. We are called to the fellowship of a gallant company, 'Ye become followers of us, and of the Lord,' wrote St. Paul to the men of Thessalonica. Who follows in their train?

"Make me Thy mountaineer;
I would not linger on the lower slope.
Fill me afresh with hope, O God of hope,
That undefeated I may climb the hill
As seeing Him who is invisible,

"Whom having not seen I love.
O my Redeemer, when this little while
Lies far behind me and the last defile
Is all alight, and in that light I see
My Saviour and my Lord, what will it be . . .?"[10]

Coping with Disappointment

There is a buoyancy in helping others, a joy in seeing the positive results of our help in their accomplishment. But each of us who in some way minister to the needs of people become at times drained, "weary in well doing," disappointed over disappointing results. This brings us pain which combines fatigue with disappointment. Referring to Demas—a biblical example of one who was led to Christ, trusted by Paul, and then who turned back—Amy Carmichael explains this pain in disappointment:

"After long prayer and toil, a soul has been led to Christ. By a thousand little signs you know that the miracle is happening for which you have waited so long. Then other influences begin to play upon that soul. Some Demas, once trusted and beloved, snatches at the chance to wound his forsaken Lord, and injects poison. The one who lately ran so well falters, looks back, goes back.

"Then comes a terrific temptation to regard that Demas with eyes which see only his Demas qualities. And, as imperceptibly as water oozes through an earthen vessel, power to expect his return to peace and purity begins to pass. When the next new inquirer comes there may be a fear to meet him with buoyant, loving hope.

"But this is fatal. Better be disappointed a thousand times—yes, and deceived—than once miss a chance to help a soul because of that faithless inhibition that grows, before we are aware of it, into suspicion and hardness. There is only one thing to be done. It is to realise that in us there is no good thing, nor faith, nor hope, nor even love; nothing human suffices here. All that we counted ours shrivels in the hot winds of disappointment: Thy servant hath not anything in the house. But the love of God suffices for any disappointment, for any defeat. And in that love is the energy of faith and the very sap of hope."[11]

When I feel that I have nothing left to give I find it helpful to realize that "nothing human suffices here." It is then time for me to turn to Him who will always fill an empty surrendered vessel with Himself.

Sometimes when I have nothing left to give, God is trying to tell me to slow down, to do less, but yet to do it more effectively. For we human beings are extremists at times, tending to overdo or to do not much at all.

Speaking of the need to slow down and produce quality, Miss Carmichael wrote:

"We must learn, as the Tamil proverb says, to plough deep rather than wide. Only God can plough both deep and wide." Then, quoting Samuel Rutherford, " 'There is but a certain quantity of spiritual force in any man. Spread it over a broad surface, the stream is shallow and languid; narrow the channel and it becomes a driving force.' "[12]

Sometimes the person who disappoints us, however, is not someone we have only ministered to but someone who has ministered to us as well. He or she is our friend, not just part of our work, and in our tiredness and discouragement we need them. Then the pain has perhaps an even greater sting.

Of this Miss Carmichael says:

"A beautiful quatrain is about silence where a disappointing friend is concerned; when those to whom we clung disappoint, keep the sad secret hid, cling to them still. The growing grain has husks; the water has its form; flowers have a scentless outer sheath of leaves."[13]

She continues: "Be careful also of your after-thinking as well as of your after-talking about any who have misjudged you. 'The hill-man thinks upon the beauty of his hills; the farmer thinks upon his fields that have yielded him rich crops; the good think on the boons bestowed by worthy men; the base man's thoughts are fixed on the abuse he has received,' is another old Tamil saying. Do not feed unloving thoughts. Remember His word, 'I forgave thee all that debt.' "[14]

And so Miss Carmichael concludes her discussion on friends with these marvelous words: "Why should we ever be bound? Of what account is anything if our King knows?"[15] Using Christ as our example is a great comfort in times of trial.

Coping with Loneliness

We live in an age of loneliness which is symbolized by a desperate clinging to the past, escape in alcohol and drugs, and unlimited numbers of group activities, created not so much out of interest in a common theme as out of a desire to meet people—all to avoid loneliness.

Amy Carmichael found an ability to cope with loneliness as she looked at Christ's life; then, to apply to her own life those principles found in Him as she struggled with health problems and loneliness in India:

"Years later, in an hour of need, the Everlasting Comforter came through the Septuagint version of Psalm cv. 18, His soul (Joseph's) entered into iron. It was not that others put him in irons (though they did, they hurt his feet with fetters), it was that he himself acquiesced in, willingly walked into the unexplained trial of his God's dealings with him. 'His soul entered, whole and entire in its resolve to obey God, into the cruel torture,' is Kay's note on that great matter; but what fathomless depths it must have held for our Lord Jesus when He set His face stedfastly to go to Jerusalem, Gethsemane, Calvary, and certain it is that whatever way of pain may open before any one of us, we find as we walk in it the marks of our dear Lord's footsteps leading on. He walked alone on that road so that we need never walk alone. No star, no flower, no song was Thine, but darkness three hours long.

"He was hard on Himself, but there is no hardness in His ways with us, and the dimmest pages in our story shine as we look back on them. We saw this once in parable. Some of us had gone to the coast to try to get rid of a persistent fever, and one night we bathed deliciously in a little bay between dark rocks. The night was moonless and starless, and the sea, except where it broke in ripples or waves, was as dark as sea can ever be. But when we came out of that water we were covered from head to foot in phosphorescent light, and when we sat down on the wet sand and dug our hands into it, diamonds ran between our fingers.

"There are lights that watch on occasion to appear. Such are the lights of strong consolation that have come when all was dark, whether because of some black trouble like the black seas of sin, or because of threatened harm or loss to that which is so much dearer to us than ourselves. For truly the love of the Lord whose brightness is as the light, who is Himself light, passeth all things for illumination, and if I say, Surely the darkness shall cover me; even the night shall be light about me."[16]

Coping with Repeated Trials

Much has been written about trial in the Christian life. Simplistically we assume that we suffer, recover and go on. Often I find that trials reoccur. Just when I thought I was finished with illness or the hurt of death or some other painful experience, it suddenly reappears.

In a chapter entitled, "And Then the Dark Wood Again" Miss Carmichael says of this second wood, this repetition of trial:

"Perhaps this second wood may find the traveller startled or depressed by a recurrence of some trial which he had thought was well behind him. 'I have not passed this way heretofore,' he had said to himself when he entered the first dark wood. 'I shall henceforth return no more that way.' Nor does he, but perhaps just after a clear vision of peace from some House Beautiful he finds confronting him something very like the dark wood of earlier days. It is in fact a further reach of that wood.

"Here is one, perhaps an athlete, who has never been ill and never contemplated illness. He has become the vassal of Eternal Love. *Look, love, and follow:* Prince Charlie engraved this motto on his seal when he came to call the clans to suffer and die for him. The words are engraved upon the life of this soldier who has looked, loved, and followed his Prince overseas. But his first year sees him handicapped by illness. He recovers, is struck down again, he who never was ill before. This repeated illness, battle-wound though it be, so unexpected, so exhausting, can appear like a very dark wood. Battle-wounds may sound heroic, but they do not feel so."[17]

Then as she continues in that same chapter: "The

call to enter for the second time into any painful experience is a sign of our Lord's confidence. It offers a great
opportunity. 'The most powerful thing in your life is
your opportunity,' said Kleobulos of Lindos; it is also the
most irretrievable. We must have clearness of vision and
courage and a quiet mind if we are to see it, and lay
hands upon it as it hurries past us on very quiet feet and
disappears as utterly as the day that has gone: 'As thy
servant was busy here and there' it was gone. God give
us vision and courage and a quiet mind."[18]

Purpose? It lies in those words: "The call to enter for
the second time into any painful experience is a sign of
our Lord's confidence." To be included as such a val-
ued servant of our Lord is to be living in the context of
eternity's values. It is to have purpose; to cope.

Sometimes in a psychotherapist's office one sees
symptoms come back that had once gone. Trauma hits
again just as one is recovering from previous trauma.
Such occurrence may be interpreted by some as a sign
of God's disapproval. Rather, should we not see this
reoccurring painful experience as an indication of God's
further opportunity for His child to trust the Lord for the
assurance and comfort He provides for traversing this
second dark wood? And what is true in the psychological realm is equally true in the physical. For physical
illness too may reoccur in the life of God's child.

Coping with Fears of Death

How often each of us must be reminded that the
eternal value of a situation does not lie in our feelings or
in what appears upon the surface. Death is one of those
experiences which we Christians feel we should not face
with fear or discomfort. Nevertheless, we can empathize

with this expression from one noted preacher who said, "I do not fear eternity but I do not look forward to the process of dying."

An Indian nurse in the missionary compound where Miss Carmichael worked was dying of cancer. Ponnammal was her name and she expressed graphically the pain of dying as well as the realism of God's sustenance. Said Miss Carmichael of this experience:

" 'Last night,' [Ponnammal] said, 'I had less pain than usual, and my mind was clear. When the confusion passes, and the power to think returns, then my heart rises as if released from a weight; I can pray and praise. But first I examined myself to be sure all was well with me. For many days I had felt nothing, not even comfort, all was dimness and a blank and silence; then as I told my God about it He showed me that all through the days the joy of His salvation was within me, unchanged by any misery of pain. It was there, but I could not taste it. The darkness and the sadness of that time was caused by the medicine; *it was not that I had lost anything.* This comforted me, and I praised Him greatly and was content.' For many days her mouth had had that drawn look which those who have nursed anyone through sore suffering will know too well. But as she talked the old sweet, satisfied look returned, and all the old happy curves were there again. 'Oh, is it not wonderful!' she exclaimed with a sort of vigorous joyousness. 'For days and nights the waves beat hard on me, and then suddenly there is a great calm, and I lie back and rest.'

"Then she asked for the last few verses of 1 Cor. 15, repeating after me the words, 'Thanks be to God, which giveth us the victory.' And then I read the 46th Psalm to her, and she fell asleep."[19] The experience was not one of the eradication of pain but rather one of coping

because of God's provision. She did not annihilate pain
and depression but she came through all of that darkness to a knowledge of God's approval.

Coping with Fears of Failure

One form of suffering which Amy Carmichael
pointed out and helped solve so realistically was the fear
of failure. All of us conjure up giants in our lives—the
"might-be's," the "what-if's." What if our child does not
grow up with our hopes and expectations? What if our
money doesn't last? What if our health gives way? What
if I end up alone and helpless in my old age? Each of us
has our own what-if's and each of us may not entirely
relate to the what-if's of our neighbor. Writes Miss
Carmichael:

"But we can be tormented by fear of failing before
the end of a journey. We need not fear. It was George
Tankervil, he who said,

'Though the day be never so long,
At last it ringeth to evensong,
Who out of weakness, was made strong.'

"He so greatly feared lest he should flinch from
martyrdom, that to test himself he had a fire kindled in
the chamber where he was confined, and sitting on a
form before it, he put off his shoes and hose and
stretched out his foot to the flame; but when it touched
his foot, 'he quickly withdrew his leg, showing how the
flesh did persuade him one way and the Spirit another
way.' And yet a few hours later, when he came to the
green place near the west end of St. Albans Abbey
where the stake was set, he kneeled down, and when he
had ended his prayer he arose with a joyful faith. Before
they put the fire to him a certain knight went near and

said softly, 'Good brother, be strong in Christ.' And he answered, 'I am so. I thank God.' So embracing the fire, he bathed himself in it, and calling on the name of the Lord, was quickly out of pain.

"Have we not often been like George Tankervil? We have imagined what was coming, and perhaps tested our constancy by some fire of our own kindling, and faith and courage have suddenly collapsed. For grace to endure and to conquer is never given till the moment of need, but when that moment comes? O Saviour, who dost not forget Thy Calvary, hast Thou ever failed the soul that trusted Thee? Never, never. By the merits of Thy Blood all is well, all shall be well."[20]

Amy Carmichael had her own what-if's. She feared that at the end of her life she would linger on to be a burden to others. Years before her death she had written in her journal: "Lord, teach me how to conquer pain to the uttermost henceforth, and grant this my earnest request. When my day's work is done, take me straight Home. Do not let me be ill and a burden or anxiety to anyone. O let me finish my course with joy and not with grief. Thou knowest there could be no joy if I knew I were tiring those whom I love best, or taking them from the children. Let me die of a battle-wound, O my Lord, not of a lingering illness."[21]

However, for years before she died, Miss Carmichael was totally bedridden. But even here she triumphed in a deep way with God and some of her special insights in writing came during those years.

During those last days she kept by her side the last stanza of an old hymn which epitomized her source of comfort:

"Green pastures are before me
Which yet I have not seen,

Bright skies will soon be o'er me
   Where the dark clouds have been.
My hope I cannot measure,
   My path to life is free,
My Saviour has my treasure,
   And He will walk with me."[22]

In all of her endeavors Christ was her motivation, her source of power, her lifetime goal. That made all the difference in her suffering.

The Constant Victory

It was a typically tropical day in a small coastal town in Mexico. I had come to rest, relax, write, yet I was still terribly tired. No book had been finished. Even my body had not responded to the rest as quickly as I had hoped. Feeling quite discouraged, but not wanting to impose that dreary feeling on my friends, I went off by myself for a while to be alone. I looked out at the ocean which was clear and blue, and felt nothing. Coconut palms and surrounding hills were green from the recent rains but they too could not meet my need. I was irritated with the fatigue and the gloom of going home and facing once again a full schedule and not enough physical strength.

Languidly I thumbed through the pages of one of my Amy Carmichael books. (I usually take one with me when I go on a trip.) My eyes fell on these words:

"For, lo, the winter is past, the rain is over and gone; the flowers appear on the earth; the time of the singing of birds is come. . . . There has been a turning of the captivity and the hard weather has passed, but there is still something stark in our landscape. . . . There is a fact, a memory, a possibility, that strikes up and faces us wherever we look. That knot of painful circumstances is there; that fear, that fearful thing, may be waiting in the

shadows to spring upon us like a panther on a fawn."[23]
Then in reference to a photograph full of the beauty of
nature, yet also including a picture of an ancient ruin
right in the middle of all the beauty, Miss Carmichael
continues:

"The picture is a figure of the true: it is full of grace
and a lovely lightness, but it is the ruin that arrests the
eye and gives character to the whole. Take it out, and
you have merely a pretty page of scenery, and life is
more than that. The charm of leaf and bud after a time of
snow is not all that God has for those whom He is
preparing to minister to others."[24]

My life, too, had its own "lovely lightness" but it had
been the "knot of painful circumstances" which had
intruded into my thinking even in this tropical paradise. I
realized afresh that "life is more than that." The pain,
the fatigue, the things I would like to erase from the
landscape of my life are those very things which God
was using to prepare me in my ministry for Him. The
challenge is that the ruin in my life, those painful things I
would like to erase, not remain a mere ruin but be
transformed by His hand into something positive.

God is in the process of bringing us to wholeness, to
completeness, that we may be totally prepared for the
fulfillment of His purposes in us. The process often
includes fierce and fearful times. There may be ruins
along the way. But we can be sure that in God's crucible
we have the promise of a glorious, shining end. In Amy
Carmichael's words:

"One day we took the children to see a goldsmith
refine gold after the ancient manner of the East. He was
sitting beside his little charcoal-fire. (He shall sit as a
refiner: the gold or silversmith never leaves his crucible

once it is on the fire.) In that red glow lay a common curved roof-tile; another tile covered it like a lid. This was the crucible. In it was the medicine made of salt, tamarind fruit and burnt brick-dust, and embedded in it was the gold. The medicine does its appointed work on the gold, 'then the fire eats it,' and the goldsmith lifts the gold out with a pair of tongs, lets it cool, rubs it between his fingers, and if not satisfied puts it back again in fresh medicine. This time he blows the fire hotter than it was before, and each time he puts the gold into the crucible the heat of the fire is increased: 'It could not bear it so hot at first, but it can bear it now; what would have destroyed it then helps it now.' 'How do you know when the gold is purified?' we asked him, and he answered, 'When I can see my face in it [the liquid gold in the crucible] then it is pure.' "[25]

Thus, when in us our Refiner sees His own image, He has indeed brought us to ultimate and true wholeness! To me this was a comforting insight.

The ocean uplifted once more. The fatigue even seemed to lift a bit as I rejoined my mind. In the back of my mind I could not quite forget Amy Carmichael's poem which summarized all of my feelings at that moment—and indeed, what this book is really all about.

"Before the winds that blow do cease,
  Teach me to dwell within Thy calm:
Before the pain has passed in peace,
  Give me, my God, to sing a psalm.
Let me not lose the chance to prove
  The fulness of enabling love,
O Love of God, do this for me:
  Maintain a constant victory.

"Before I leave the desert land
  For meadows of immortal flowers,
Lead me where streams at Thy command
  Flow by the borders of the hours,
That when the thirsty come, I may
  Show them the fountains in the way.
O Love of God, do this for me:
  Maintain a constant victory."[26]

Notes

All material quoted is used by permission.

1. Frank Houghton, *Amy Carmichael of Dohnavur* (Fort Washington, PA: Christian Literature Crusade, n.d.), p. 195.
2. Amy Carmichael, *Toward Jerusalem* (Fort Washington, PA: Christian Literature Crusade, 1961), p. 94.
3. Amy Carmichael, *Kohila* (Fort Washington, PA: Christian Literature Crusade, n.d.), p. 129.
4. Ibid., pp. 129,130.
5. Ibid., pp. 131,132.
6. Amy Carmichael, *Gold by Moonlight* (Fort Washington, PA: Christian Literature Crusade, 1960), p. 48.
7. Ibid., p. 46.
8. Carmichael, *Kohila*, p. 97.
9. Amy Carmichael, *Rose from Brier* (Fort Washington, PA: Christian Literature Crusade, 1972), pp. 18,19.
10. Carmichael, *Gold by Moonlight*, pp. 74,75.
11. Amy Carmichael, *Gold Cord* (Fort Washington, PA: Christian Literature Crusade, 1957), p. 139.
12. Carmichael, *Kohila*, p. 139.
13. Ibid., p. 134.
14. Ibid., p. 135.
15. Ibid., p. 136.
16. Carmichael, *Gold Cord*, pp. 169,170.
17. Carmichael, *Gold by Moonlight*, p. 93.
18. Ibid., pp. 101,102.
19. Amy Carmichael, *Ponnammal* (Fort Washington, PA: Christian Literature Crusade, 1950), pp. 108,109.
20. Carmichael, *Rose from Brier*, pp. 112,113.
21. Houghton, *Amy Carmichael*, p. 189.
22. Ibid., p. 373.
23. Carmichael, *Gold by Moonlight*, p. 36.
24. Ibid., p. 38.
25. Carmichael, *Gold Cord*, pp. 69,70.
26. Carmichael, *Rose from Brier*, p. XII.

CHAPTER 4

Coping with Human Needs

An Insight into the Life of Hudson Taylor

It was late spring. The weather was beginning to warm up and once again I began my frequent visits to the ocean. This year it was different, however. I had just started a new career. I was building a private counseling practice, after teaching school for 12 years. Until that practice expanded I had plenty of time to go to the beach—and to think. I kept remembering that I had given up a fixed income, paid sick leave and vacations and general security in exchange for the unknown. Unknown, that is, except that God had led me; so the way was known at least to Him.

It was sunset as I drove home from the beach on a street overlooking the sea and shaded by large trees. Waves of doubt caused me to feel restless and a little frantic. How would I live until I had time to build up the

practice? What if I didn't make it financially? Then, with
as much reality as that deepening sunset, there flashed
across my mind the thoughts of a passage in Scripture:

"Ye cannot be in service unto God and unto riches.
For this cause I say unto you: Be not anxious for your life
what ye shall eat or what ye shall drink, or for your body
what ye shall put on: Is not the life more than food? And
the body more than raiment? Observe intently the birds
of the heaven, that they neither sow nor reap nor gather
into barns, and yet your heavenly Father feedeth them:
Are not ye much better than they?

"But who from among you, being anxious can add
to his stature one cubit? And about clothing why are ye
anxious? Consider well the lilies of the field how they
grow,—They toil not neither do they spin; and yet I say
unto you not even Solomon in all his glory was arrayed
like one of these!

"Now if the grass of the field—which today is and
tomorrow into an oven is cast—God thus adorneth not
much rather you little of faith?

"Do not then be anxious saying, What shall we eat?
Or What shall we drink? Or Wherewithal shall we be
arrayed?

"For all these things the nations seek after,—For
your heavenly Father knoweth that ye are needing all
these things. But be seeking first the kingdom and its
righteousness—And all these things shall be added unto
you" (Matt. 6:24-33, *The Emphasized Bible*).

In my own words, I knew that God would provide
for me in an undertaking which had been instigated at
His prodding. Where there had been fear there was now
peace and a sense of excitement over how and when
God would work. That frame of mind does not come to

me easily, so I knew that it had surely come from God.

Similarly, a year ago I spent some time in a small primitive town in Mexico. It is a place of exquisite beauty and peace. It is also remote from modern medical help and therefore not the best place to become ill. One morning I woke up with what I knew was more than a simple case of Montezuma's Revenge. I was sick and feverish. Because I am sufficiently allergic to most medication, I wanted to avoid any local cures.

As I lay in bed that afternoon I calmly asked God to heal me. A logical request since I firmly believed that God's purposes for my life were still alive and real and that they required health. The result was a shaky but increasing return to physical well-being by that evening.

I do not believe that God unfailingly answers our prayers for healing with an answer of yes. Sometimes He says no or wait. Or, He chooses to give partial help. But at a time when I was without usable medical attention God undertook to do the whole job Himself, an experience that was very bolstering to my faith in future days. God had provided for my needs as my life was centered in His will. He had not prevented my illness nor did He eliminate illness on future trips to Mexico. But He did provide for my physical needs. He helped me cope. He healed when that was necessary. God is not in the business of eradicating our problems, but He is definitely the One who supplies our needs in the middle of those problems.

God's Supply for God's Work

Hudson Taylor, the man who almost single-handedly opened up the interior of China to Christianity, learned first as a young preacher in England, a principle of God's provision: "God's work done in God's way will never lack God's supply." One might add to that: "God's person, bent on doing God's will, shall have God's supply."

To Hudson Taylor a significant beginning in this life of trusting God for all practical supply came late one evening: "After concluding my last service about ten o'clock that night, a poor man asked me to go and pray with his wife, saying that she was dying. I readily agreed, and on the way asked him why he had not sent for the priest, as his accent told me he was an Irishman. He had done so, he said, but the priest refused to come without a payment of eighteen pence, which the man did not possess as the family was starving. Immediately it occurred to my mind that all the money I had in the world was the solitary half-crown, and that was in one coin; moreover, that while the basin of water-gruel I usually took for supper was awaiting me, and there was sufficient in the house for breakfast in the morning, I certainly had nothing for dinner on the coming day.

"Somehow or other there was at once a stoppage in the flow of joy in my heart. But instead of reproving myself I began to reprove the poor man, telling him that it was very wrong to have allowed matters to get into such a state as he described, and that he ought to have applied to the relieving officer. His answer was that he had done so, and was told to come at eleven o'clock the next morning, but that he feared his wife might not live through the night.

" 'Ah,' thought I, 'if only I had two shillings and a sixpence instead of this half-crown, how gladly would I give these poor people a shilling!' But to part with the half-crown was far from my thoughts. I little dreamed that the truth of the matter simply was that I could trust God plus *one-and-sixpence,* but was not prepared to trust Him only, without any money at all in my pocket.

"My conductor led me into a court, down which I followed him with some degree of nervousness. I had found myself there before, and at my last visit had been roughly handled . . . . Up a miserable flight of stairs into a wretched room he led me, and oh what a sight there presented itself! Four or five children stood about, their sunken cheeks and temples telling unmistakably the story of slow starvation, and lying on a wretched pallet was a poor, exhausted mother, with a tiny infant thirty-six hours old moaning rather than crying at her side.

" 'Ah!' thought I, 'If I had two shillings and a six-pence, instead of half-a-crown, how gladly should they have one-and-sixpence of it.' But still a wretched unbelief prevented me from obeying the impulse to relieve their distress at the cost of all I possessed.

"It will scarcely seem strange that I was unable to say much to comfort these poor people. I needed comfort myself. I began to tell them, however, that they must not be cast down; that though their circumstances were very distressing there was a kind and loving Father in heaven. But something within me cried, 'You hypocrite! Telling these unconverted people about a kind and loving Father in heaven and not prepared yourself to trust Him without half-a-crown.'

"I nearly choked. How gladly would I have compromised with conscience, if I had had a florin and sixpence! I would have given the florin thankfully and kept the rest. But I was not yet prepared to trust in God alone, without the sixpence.

"To talk was impossible under these circumstances,

yet strange to say, prayer was a delightful occupation in those days. Time thus spent never seemed wearisome and I knew no lack of words. I seemed to think that all I should have to do would be to kneel down and pray, and that relief would come to them and to myself together."[1]

Perhaps at this time in his life Taylor began to learn on a deep gut level that God does not usually work in such a simplistic way. He cooperates with us to work out the meeting of our needs rather than just eliminating those needs. And thus we grow and learn to trust God more.

In his process of learning this trust, Taylor continued:

" 'You asked me to come and pray with your wife,' I said to the man; 'let us pray.' And I knelt down.

"But no sooner had I opened my lips with, 'Our Father who art in heaven,' than conscience said within, 'Dare you mock God? Dare you kneel down and call Him "Father" with that half-crown in your pocket?'

"Such a time of conflict then came upon me as I had never experienced before. How I got through that form of prayer I know not, and whether the words uttered were connected or disconnected. But I arose from my knees in great distress of mind.

"The poor father turned to me and said, 'You see what a terrible state we are in, sir. If you can help us, for God's sake do!'

"At that moment the word flashed into my mind, 'Give to him that asketh of thee.' And in the word of a King there is power.

"I put my hand into my pocket and slowly drawing out the half-crown gave it to the man, telling him that it might seem a small matter for me to relieve them, seeing that I was comparatively well off, but that in parting with that coin I was giving him my all; but that what I had been trying to tell them was indeed true, God really was a Father and might be trusted. And how the joy came back in full tide to my heart! I could say anything and feel it then, and the hindrance to blessing was gone—gone, I trust, forever.

"Not only was the poor woman's life saved, but my life as I fully realized had been saved too. It might have been a wreck . . . had not grace at that time conquered and the striving of God's Spirit been obeyed.

"I well remember that night as I went home to my lodgings how my heart was as light as my pocket. The dark, deserted streets resounded with a hymn of praise that I could not restrain. When I took my basin of gruel before retiring, I would not have exchanged it for a prince's feast. Reminding the Lord as I knelt at my bedside of His own Word, 'He that giveth to the poor lendeth to the Lord,' I asked Him not to let my loan be a long one, or I should have no dinner the next day. And with peace within and peace without, I spent a happy, restful night.

"Next morning my plate of porridge remained for breakfast, and before it was finished the postman's knock was heard at the door. I was not in the habit of receiving letters on Monday, as my parents and most of my friends refrained from posting on Saturday, so that I was somewhat surprised when the landlady came in holding a letter or packet in her wet hand covered by her apron. I looked at the letter, but could not make out the handwriting. It was either a strange hand or a feigned one, and the postmark was blurred. Where it came from

I could not tell. On opening the envelope I found nothing written within, but inside a sheet of blank paper was folded a pair of kid gloves from which, as I opened them in astonishment, half-a-soverign fell to the ground."[2]

Principles of God's Supply

God's work done in God's way had received God's supply. Need had not been eradicated, for there will always be great need on this earth. The need had been supplied, which is a basic principle of God's work.

In all accuracy it should be added that Taylor lived in an economy different than ours. Additionally one must glean from great lives *principles* of living rather than strict dogma. Furthermore, it is dangerous to become a carbon copy of anyone.

To illustrate, I know an elderly lady who gave all she possessed to a radio broadcast under the duress of questioning her loyalty to God unless she so gave. A few months later she was living in misery with the grudging help of some relatives.

Each one of us must consider his or her finances in the light of God's will for our individual lives—each with its own needs.

There is another principle of truth to be gleaned, however, from Taylor's experience with the coin. As he himself expressed it, "If we are faithful to God in little things, we shall gain experience and strength that will be helpful to us in the more serious trials of life." More than that, God's training is unique for each of us. Taylor's "more serious trials of life" later, in China, forced him to the extreme of faith. The loss of his wife and children, and loss of his missionary co-workers were all to weigh heavily upon this man. At these times he would pace his study for hours, calming himself as he softly sang, "Jesus! I am resting, resting in the joy of what Thou art. I am finding out the greatness of Thy loving heart." Truly "the life that was to be exceptionally fruitful had to be rooted and grounded in God in no ordinary way."[3]

It was in experiences such as that of the coin that Hudson Taylor learned what George Müller had also learned: *God's work can be done expansively and with quality, and we can expect God's supply.* The needs would never go away. They would remain constant and daily. But they would unfailingly be met in God's way and in God's time.

God's Expansive Supply

In Taylor's founding of the China Inland Mission— perhaps one of the greatest foreign missions—Taylor brought together deeply dedicated Christians who gave and were given to. They gave up this world's goods. Yet years later, for example, when Geraldine Taylor (Hudson's daughter-in-law and biographer) was in need of rest in the middle of her writing, she was sent to a lovely ocean resort for six months—with household help! And she should have been.

Individual saints must consider their finances, however, in the light of God's will for *their* life with *its* needs. Sometimes God asks for a plunge of faith financially. Then do it! Sometimes He asks for hard core common sense. Then use it! An older person lovingly cared for by five adult children *may* be more generous financially than one who has no living relative. Hudson Taylor in his youth, also could more rationally give away his last coin than perhaps a Taylor facing open heart surgery for his child or the poverty of his parents. For it is a biblical principle that one should care for those of his own household first. Apart from direct Christian teaching, this principle is considered valid in most people's thinking.

In commenting upon the absolute degradation and ruin of the Ik, a tribe in Uganda, and applying his conclusions to the Western world, Anthropologist Colin Turnbull says: "The rot is in all of us, for how many of us would be willing to divide our riches among our own family, let alone the poor or needy, beyond, of course, what we can easily afford—for if we were willing, why have we not done it?"[4] Should those in the Body of Christ have lower standards?

On this principle Müller built orphanages which excelled all others in England at that time. For Müller believed that if God's work was to be done, it was to be done well. Reports of Müller's success greatly influenced the life of Hudson Taylor in China and that of Amy Carmichael in Dohnavur in her work with children rescued from the temples of South India. Taylor, Müller, and Carmichael held several of the same basic principles—with Müller as a major influence on the other two. Predominant was their conviction that God's work done in God's way would receive God's supply.

They believed a second principle: that one could move people by prayer alone, which meant that no pledges were signed, no financial pleas expressed.

And certainly not least, they each believed that if they were in the employment of a King, the work could afford to have quality. Since Müller's success based on these principles was dramatic, was influential on the work of God throughout the world, and is pertinent to us today, a lengthy quote of his work is appropriate in connection with our thoughts of God's provision.

A visitor to Müller's orphanage observed in detail the following:

"On entering the grounds in which two of the houses stand, we passed the lodge, a neat little cottage on the right, and proceeded along the pathway by the side of the carriage-drive, which, together with a well-trimmed lawn, and some pretty flowerbeds, separates No. 1 House from No. 2. There are large pieces of ground surrounding each of the houses, devoted to the cultivation of vegetables. The perfect order and neatness characterizing everything outside the establishment gave us a good intimation of what we might expect within; nor were we disappointed.

"The Orphan House No. 1, which contains usually 140 girls above seven years of age, 80 boys of the same age, and 80 infants of either sex, was that we first visited; but in describing it we shall follow that order which seems best fitted to give a clear understanding of the establishment, and not that in which the different parts are—to save time—shown to visitors.

"There are three school-rooms—boys', girls', and infants'—all large, airy, cheerful-looking apartments. The girls', which is shown first of the three, is very spacious and lofty, situated on the ground-floor, and well fitted up with the best modern maps and other helps for learning. As our party, numbering some sixty or seventy, entered, we beheld about one hundred and twenty girls, sitting at work at low desks; all clothed alike in blue print frocks and neat pinafores, and with their hair cut short behind, but arranged with the greatest neatness. On a signal from the principal teacher, who was stationed on a small platform, with a desk in front, the girls all stood up and placed their hands behind them. At another signal one of the orphans struck up a cheerful song, which the rest at once joined in, and all marched out in single file, with as much precision in their steps as any of our modern volunteer corps would exhibit. The effect of this sight was really very striking; and he who can witness unmoved these helpless orphans winding their way between the desks, to the music of the touching songs which they sang, one after another, must indeed be made of very impenetrable materials. As they passed round the ends of the desks in front of the visitors, who lined the walls on either side, I looked carefully at the features of each child, and, although in some cases I saw evident traces of disease, inherited, doubtless, from the parents whom they had lost, still there was a general appearance of health and cheerfulness in their happy faces.

"Then we were taken to the girls' 'cloak and shoe room,' where we found a vast number of serviceable plaid cloaks hanging up around the room, for winter wear. Each girl, too, has three pairs of shoes for use—a mark of sound economy on Mr. Müller's part, as every *paterfamilias* well knows."

Continuing, the report provides more details which point out not only God's supply, but even more particularly the quality of that supply:

"The boys' school-room does not materially differ from that of the girls. There were, at our entrance, about 80 boys seated at desks, dressed all alike in blue cloth jackets and corduroy trousers. Their appearance was certainly that of vigorous health. They looked sturdy, good-tempered fellows. At the word of command they all rose from their seats, and marched one after another between the desks to the air of some spirited song, just as the girls had before. Two separate rooms are appropriated as work-rooms also—one for the boys, and one for the girls; the former are taught, a few at a time, to knit and mend their own stockings, and the girls to make their own garments, under the superintendence of a teacher who does the cutting out for them. Then come the play-rooms, one for boys and another for girls. These are large, lofty rooms, with a few low forms, and nothing else in the shape of furniture. These are, of course, only intended for use in bad weather, at least in the case of the boys. For there is a capital court for playing in for each class of orphans, and swings and other apparatus for exercise and play. The girls' playroom was provided with large cupboards, divided into small pigeon-holes, one for each child, well stored with dolls, dolls' houses, and a variety of other toys, the gifts, sometimes of relatives (who are allowed to visit the orphans once a month), sometimes of ladies, who present them to the teachers to be used as rewards.

"The infant department in the Orphan House never fails to arrest the attention of visitors. Would that we could adequately bring before the reader the "infant school," with its two hundred little ones, or nearly so—many not more than three years of age.

"We must say a few words about the 'infant nursery.' Some infants, it should be remembered, are taken in so young that they are literally *babies,* and these are nursed in a small comfortable room by a motherly-looking head nurse, assisted by two or three of the elder girls. It was a touching sight to watch these helpless infants toddling about with pretty horses or dolls in their hands, and some in the arms of their nurses. Around the room, too, we noticed several little basket beds in which these tiny babies might be placed, when overcome with sleep, with all the fondness of a mother's love."

Again emphasizing the quality with which God's work can and must be done, the narrative continues:

"Many visitors seem to regard as one of the prettiest sights in the whole establishment the 'infants' wardrobe.' It was a room about twenty feet long, and ranged on each side of the room stood painted deal presses, divided into small pigeon-holes, in each of which were laid by, neatly folded up, small duplicates of all the various articles of clothing worn by the infants. The one side was set apart for the girls' wardrobes, each little pile of clothing being crowned by a pretty little straw bonnet, and each garment being most carefully and neatly rolled up and pinned together. On the opposite side stood the same number of presses for the boys' clothes, and on the top of each tiny wardrobe that occupied the pigeon-holes, there was placed a little blue cloth cap. It is a fact, that scarcely any part of the house affects strangers so much as this infants' wardrobe; and it is a common thing to see tears in the eyes of one and another of the visitors, as they gaze on the exquisite order and nicety which prevail on every side, and think of the tender love which had so wonderfully cared for the smallest wants of these helpless little ones.

"Next to the infants' wardrobe room comes the infants' dormitory. At the end of the dormitory is a passage on each side of which are situated the private rooms of the matrons and teachers. These were most comfortably furnished, and quite in keeping with the station of those who occupy such positions in the Orphan Houses. Each individual has a separate apartment.

"The infants' dormitory, to which we have referred, is a spacious room, with abundance of air and light—filled with little tiny bedsteads. These are all of iron, painted of a light yellow color, and many fitted round with railings to preserve the younger babes from falling out. The beds are ranged in three rows from one end of the room to the other. There is no other article of furniture in the room of any description. Four larger beds—two at each end of the room—are occupied by the elder girls who take charge of the forty little orphans who nightly sleep in this cheerful room. Forty other infant orphans occupy the corresponding room to this, which we were afterwards shown.

"There is a third bed-room for girls, in which 140 female orphans sleep—two girls occupying one bed. The same marvelous cleanliness of floors, and spotless purity of quilts and bed-clothes, with which our party was so impressed in the infants' dormitory, strikes us here. One good woman, in the height of her amazement, exclaimed, looking at the well-scrubbed boards, "Why, you might eat your dinner off them!" Another visitor, of the opposite sex, whose face was an index to the benevolence which filled his heart, observed, as he gazed at the beds, with the bed-clothes folded down with the utmost nicety and precision: 'Ah, they would never have slept in such beds if their parents had lived!' Great indeed was the admiration which this comfortable apartment elicited from our party. But it is impossible to describe the effect with pen and ink; it must be seen to be understood. At the end of the room there is a small window, opening into a bed-room occupied by one of the teachers, who is thus enabled to overlook the movements of the children. We afterwards saw the dormitories for boys, which it is unnecessary to describe, as they correspond exactly with the one just mentioned, except that only forty children sleep in each. Besides these, there is a small dormitory with eight beds in it for the elder girls, usually called "house-girls," as they are engaged in house-work, and are on the point of being sent out to service. Each of these has the privilege of a good strong box to hold her clothes in. These girls daily assist the servants in the general work of the house.

"After we had seen the infants' wardrobes, we were invited to inspect two other wardrobe rooms. The first we came to was the boys'. The arrangement of this room exactly agreed with that containing the infants' clothes. Each boy has a square compartment, in which to keep his clothes, with his number marked, in one of the large deal presses that line the room. Six boys, we were told, are draughted out to take charge of the wardrobes, and see that everything is kept in proper order. When their term of service is expired, their place is supplied by six others, until each boy in the house, of a fit age, has taken his turn. The boys have each three suits of clothes. The girls' wardrobe room corresponded with that for the boys, except that it is much larger. There were the same lofty painted deal presses, subdivided into innumerable little pigeon-holes. The girls have five changes of dress. Three blue print frocks for ordinary wear in the house, a lilac pattern dress for Sundays during the summer months, and a brown merino dress for winter wear. The girls make and mend all their own clothes. Six girls in rotation take charge of all the female wardrobes of the house; just as in the case of the boys.

"The dining-room where all the orphans take their meals is a spacious apartment filled with long narrow tables and forms, all as white almost as the paper on which the reader's eye is now fixed. While we were inspecting this room, we noticed some of the elder girls employed in spreading the snow-white table-cloths for the evening meal. Others at the same time entered the room with trays loaded with bread-and-butter. Soon afterwards, some hundreds of cups filled with milk-and-water were placed upon the tables; but the orphans were not called to tea until after the visitors had left."[5]

God's work was done in God's way and did receive God's supply!

A Chain of Supply

There is an incident which shows the remarkable, God-given relationship between Taylor and Müller.

A servant had made off with Mr. Taylor's belongings and proof was given. Says Geraldine Taylor:

"For the recovery of the property it would not have been difficult to institute legal proceedings, and Mr. Taylor has strongly urged to secure the punishment of the thief; but the more he thought about it the more he shrank from anything of the sort.

"Yoh-hsi was one whose salvation he had earnestly sought, and to hand him over to cruel, rapacious underlings who would only be too glad to throw him into prison that he might be squeezed of the last farthing would not have been in keeping, he felt, with the spirit of the Gospel. Finally concluding that his soul was worth more than the forty pounds worth of things he had stolen, Mr. Taylor decided to pursue a very different course.

" 'So I have sent him a plain, faithful letter,' he wrote in the middle of August, 'to the effect that we know his guilt, and what its consequences might be to himself; that at first I had considered handing over the matter to the Ya-men, but remembering Christ's command to return good for evil I had not done so, and did not wish to injure a hair of his head.

" 'I told him that he was the real loser, not I; that I freely forgave him, and besought him more earnestly than ever to flee from the wrath to come. I also added that though it was not likely he would give up such of my possessions as were serviceable to a Chinese, there were among them foreign books and papers that could be of no use to him but were valuable to me, and that those at least he ought to send back.

" 'If only his conscience might be moved and his soul saved, how infinitely more important that would be than the recovery of all I have lost. Do pray for him.'

"In course of time, and far away in England, this letter came into hands for which it had never been intended. Mr. George Müller from Bristol, founder of the well-known Orphan Homes, read it with thankfulness to God, finding in the circumstances an exemplification of the teachings of the Lord Himself. His sympathies were drawn out to the young missionary who had acted in what he felt to be a Christ-like spirit, and from that time Hudson Taylor had an interest in his prayers.

"But more than this. As soon as the incident became known to him, he sent straight out to China a sum sufficient to cover Mr. Taylor's loss, continuing thereafter to take a practical share in his work, until in a time of

special need he was used of God as the principal channel of support to the China Inland Mission. And all this
grew out of one little act, as it might seem, of loyalty to
the Master at some personal cost. Only there are no little
acts when it is a question of faithfulness to God. And it
was just his simple adherence, in every detail, to
Scriptural principles that gradually inspired confidence
in Hudson Taylor and his methods, and won for the
Mission the support of spiritually minded people in
many lands."[6]

The incident reflects the principles upon which both
Taylor and Müller stood, their respect for each other,
and, for the purposes of this book, the *man* Hudson
Taylor.

Hudson Taylor did not only emphasize God's ability
to meet the needs of God's work. He was also deeply
committed to the principle that God's work was to be
done with quality, and that while the quality would at
times be more costly, the needs would be met *because*
they were needs sanctioned by God. Faith was the
focus. Not faith abstractly without an object, but faith
that God could be trusted with great tasks. For certainly
one who serves a King should expect a King's supply as
long as he operates under a King's command. And
wisely our King has chosen often to supply us daily,
momently, rather than taking away our needs. For the
daily need is what keeps the focus of direction and faith
upon Him and His orders.

God, too, had given Hudson Taylor great training
for his life of balance in obtaining God's supply. For as
the son of James Taylor he had the perfect pattern for
learning both financial wisdom and godly trust.

Taylor was born to James and Amelia Taylor on

May 21, 1832. He lived during the years of Charles Haddon Spurgeon, and, as has been pointed out, shared ideals with Amy Carmichael and George Müller. Interestingly enough, to balance out the abandon with which Hudson Taylor gave money and trusted God financially, he was no fanatic. His father's upbringing was deeply entrenched in him and is epitomized in the statement James Taylor once made regarding a bill:

"If I let it stand over a week," he would say, "I defraud my creditor of interest, if only a fractional sum."[7]

James Taylor was a business man. Yet he never sued for a bill. And at times he returned in whole or in part sums that his customers could not afford. Still he was a man of so much business skill that his fellow townsmen who recognized his financial skill appointed him manager of their Building Society for a term of 22 years. It was in such an atmosphere of balance, integrity and faith that Hudson Taylor was born and grew.

Perhaps it was because he had such balance that he could afford to appear unbalanced to the world, even the Christian world. That too was faith. In such matters as dress his faith and sincerity were put to the acid test.

"Chinese dress and a home somewhere in the country—the thought was becoming familiar. But it was an expedient almost unheard of in those days. Sometimes on inland journeys a missionary would wear the native costume as a precautionary measure. But it was invariably discarded on the traveller's return, and he would have been careless of public opinion indeed who would have ventured to wear it always, and in the Settlement.

"But it was nothing less than this that the young

missionary was meditating, driven to it by his longing to identify himself with the people and by the force of outward circumstances. If he could not find quarters in Shanghai he *must* go to the interior, and why add to his difficulties and hinder the work he most desired to accomplish by emphasizing the fact that he was a foreigner?"8

Again Taylor had an intricate balance in his life. Chinese dress was a key to his success in China. He became part of the people in a deeper way, not only because by this sign they could observe his sincerity, but because Chinese dress helped him blend into the culture rather than stand out. By his compromise in dress Taylor met the Chinese people.

Compromise has come to be a dirty word in the Christian world, although it was indeed never meant to be that. The word has become abused in our culture. Enthusiastic do-gooders smoke pot in order to reach drug addicts or in general prostitute their principles in order to fit in with those whom they wish to help. Taylor would not have compromised principle in order to save his life, nor should we. But he knew the true meaning of compromise. In order to cope in China, he compromised things that had no moral overtones in order to win the very souls of people. He chanced offending his own colleagues rather than offend those among whom he lived and worked.

"Yes, it was growing clearer. For him, probably, the right thing was a closer identification with the people; Chinese dress at all times and the externals of Chinese life, including chop-sticks and native cookery. How much it would simplify travelling in the interior! Already he had purchased an outfit of native clothing. If, after all the prayer there had been about it, he really could not get accommodation in Shangai, it must be that the Lord had other purposes.

"Thursday night came. It was useless to seek premises any longer, so Hudson Taylor went down to engage the junk that was to take them to Hang-chow Bay with their belongings. His Chinese dress was ready for the following morning when he expected to begin a pilgrim life indeed.

"And this, apparently, was the point to which it had been necessary to lead him. He had followed faithfully. It was enough. And now on these new lines could be given the answer to weeks and months of prayer.

"Later he took the step he had been prayerfully considering—called in a barber, and had himself so transformed in appearance that his own mother could hardly have known him. To put on Chinese dress without shaving the head is comparatively a simple matter; but Hudson Taylor went [to] all lengths, leaving only enough of the fair, curly hair to grow into the *queue* of the Chinaman. He had prepared a dye, moreover, with which he darkened his remaining hair, to match the long, black braid that at first must do duty for his own. Then in the morning he put on as best he might the loose, unaccustomed garments, and appeared for the first time in the gown and satin shoes of a 'Teacher,' or man of the scholarly class."[9]

As the work went on by faith, Taylor received what he needed, not always *as* he wanted or *when* it was desirable.

A note dated January 27, 1874, found in the margin of his Bible reflects the proportion of his vision and the urgency of his need:

"Asked God for fifty or a hundred additional native evangelists and as many missionaries as may be needed to open up the four *Fu's* and forty-eight *Hsien* cities still unoccupied in Chekiang, also for men to break into the nine unoccupied provinces. Asked in the name of Jesus.

"I thank Thee, Lord Jesus, for the promise whereon Thou has given me to rest. Give me all needed strength of body, wisdom of mind, grace of soul to do this Thy so great work."[10]

"Yet, strange to say, the immediate sequel was not added strength, but a serious illness. Week after week he lay in helpless suffering, only able to hold on in faith to the heavenly vision. Funds had been so low for months that he had scarcely known how to distribute the little that came in, and there was nothing at all in hand for extension work. But, "we are going on to the interior," he had written to the secretaries in London. "I do so hope to see some of the destitute provinces evangelized before long. I long for it by day and pray for it by night. *Can he care less?*"

Faith again was required to clarify its focus. The work was God's, Taylor was God's—and God would not fail. Taylor continued:

"Never had advance seemed more impossible. But in the Bible before him was the record of that transaction of his soul with God, and in his heart was the conviction that, even for inland China, God's time had almost come. And then as he lay there slowly recovering, a letter was put into his hands which had been two months on its way from England. It was from an unknown correspondent.

"My dear Sir (the somewhat trembling hand had written), *I bless God*—in two months I hope to place at the disposal of your Council, for further extension of the China Inland Mission work, eight hundred pounds. (Then equal to about four thousand dollars, gold.) Please remember for *fresh* provinces. . . .

"I think your receipt-form beautiful: 'The Lord our Banner'; 'The Lord will provide.' If faith is put forth and praise sent up, I am sure that Jehovah of Hosts will honour it.

"Eight hundred pounds for 'fresh provinces'! Hardly could the convalescent believe he read aright. The very secrets of his heart seemed to look back at him from that sheet of foreign note paper. Even before the prayer [had been] recorded in his Bible, that letter had been sent off; and now, just when most needed, it had reached him with its wonderful confirmation. Then God's time had surely come!"11

And all that was true of the mission was true of God's provision for Hudson Taylor the man. For God cares about His work but He is not some mechanistic Task-master who is not interested in people for themselves. Let us not forget that we are indeed an extremely important possession of God and His care is never removed from us.

Said Taylor in a letter to his sister:

"The sweetest part, if one may speak of one part being sweeter than another, is the *rest* which full identification with Christ brings. I am no longer anxious about anything, as I realise this; for He, I know is able to carry out *His Will*, and His will is mine. It makes no matter where He places me, or how. That is rather for Him to consider than for me; for in the easiest positions He must give me His grace, and in the most difficult His grace is sufficient. It little matters to my servant whether I send him to buy a few cash worth of things, or the most expensive articles. In either case he looks to me for the money, and brings me his purchases. So, if God place me in great perplexity, must He not give me much guidance; in position of great difficulty, much grace; in circumstances of great pressure and trial, much strength? No fear that His resources will be unequal to the emergency! And His resources are mine, for *He* is mine, and is with me and dwells in me. All this springs from the believer's oneness with Christ. And since Christ has thus dwelt in my heart by faith, how happy I have been! I wish I could tell you, instead of writing about it."[12]

On a deeper, more personal level: After sending home two small sons and a daughter to England for health reasons, Mrs. Taylor gave birth to another son. One week later the baby died as a result of Mrs. Taylor's attack of cholera. At the age of 33, slightly over a week later, Mrs. Taylor died too. It seemed that all earthly comfort had been taken from Taylor, for within two months Taylor's youngest child hung between life and death and had to be sent to friends in another province.

In a letter to Miss Blatchley, the guardian of the other three children, Mr. Taylor's feelings are shown most tellingly:

"You will love them all the more," he wrote, "now that they can never again know a mother's care. God will help you to bear with them, and to try to correct them by lovingly pointing out the right way rather than by too frequent reproof—'Don't do this or that.' This I feel is where I most failed with them; and now, there is only you to make up for my deficiencies."[13]

Unburdened

During this time Taylor himself was almost destroyed physically. He had a badly "deranged liver" which brought on sleeplessness and painful depression. Says Geraldine Taylor: "He had to learn more than ever before of the close and often humbling connection between the one and the other (mind and body)." Lung problems and newly enforced bachelorhood did not help his condition. Yet the work went on. Taylor went on.

And Taylor's attitude of life is best epitomized in a brief incident:

"Despite absence from home and loved ones, and the limitations of ill-health which he was feeling keenly, Mr. Taylor was enabled so to cast his burdens on the Lord that, as he wrote to Mr. Hill in February (1877), he 'could not but rejoice seven days a week.' Whenever work permitted, he was in the habit of turning to a little harmonium for refreshment, playing and singing many a favourite hymn, but always coming back to:

" 'Jesus, I am resting, resting in the joy of what
    Thou art;
    I am finding out the greatness of Thy loving
    heart.'

"Some around him could hardly understand this joy and rest, especially when fellow-workers were in danger. A budget of letters arriving on one occasion, as Mr. Nicoll relates, brought news of serious rioting in two different stations. Standing at his desk to read them, Mr. Taylor mentioned what was happening and that immediate help was necessary. Feeling that he might wish to be alone, the younger man was about to withdraw, when, to his surprise, some one began to whistle. It was the soft refrain of the same well-loved hymn: 'Jesus, I am resting, resting, in the joy of what Thou art . . .'

"Turning back, Mr. Nicoll could not help exclaiming, 'How *can* you whistle, when our friends are in such danger!'

" 'Would you have me anxious and troubled?' was the long-remembered answer. 'That would not help them, and would certainly incapacitate me for my work. I have just to roll the burden on the Lord.' "

Taylor was not tranquilized into oblivion by his spiritual support. His pain was not obliterated by God. But he was enabled to cope by the very presence of God Himself. He could and did go on. He survived. He was not destroyed.

"Day and night that was his secret, 'just to roll the burden on the Lord.' Frequently those who were wakeful in the little house at Chin-kiang might hear, at two or three o'clock in the morning, the soft refrain of Mr. Taylor's favourite hymn. He had learned that, for him, only one life was possible—just that blessed life of resting and rejoicing in the Lord under all circumstances, while He dealt with the difficulties inward and outward, great and small."[14]

Of such was the fiber of Hudson Taylor, the China Inland Mission and all those connected with it. In every aspect of life there was God's provision.

My favorite picture in my family photograph album is of my Aunt Ruth dressed in a padded Chinese gown holding a lamb in one arm and a baby in the other.

I met Aunt Ruth when I was three at a train station in Chicago when she first returned from her work in the far north of China with the China Inland Mission. I remember as a child remembers: chopsticks; tiny Chinese shoes from before the days when footbinding was abandoned; strange foods that tasted good; brass bowls with Chinese dragons; a Bible with strange Chinese writing. She taught me how to hold a Chinese brush and grind Chinese ink. She taught me to count in Chinese. Above all, she taught me to love the Chinese people.

I remember lots of doctors and tests and bottles of food supplements which she took constantly to build her up. I know now that she suffered from malnutrition and needed much medical help.

I remember names like D.E. Hoste, Howard Taylor and most of all, Hudson Taylor. I remember the China Inland Mission, and the endless photographs and slides. Theirs were common names to me then. Now I know they were not common at all—not even in my life. They became a major formative influence in all of my ideals and aspirations. Years later I found on my own—or perhaps I had just forgotten—the hymn:

"Jesus! I am resting, resting,
    In the joy of what Thou art;
I am finding out the greatness
    Of Thy loving heart.
Thou hast bid me gaze upon Thee,
    And Thy beauty fills my soul,
For, by Thy transforming power,
    Thou hast made me whole."

Hudson Taylor's favorite hymn. Then my Aunt's. Now mine.

I may never know how much Hudson Taylor and his belief in God's provision have influenced me. Maybe he, too, was part of that great cloud of witnesses on that warm sunny day as I was coming home from the beach. For it was then that I knew God's provision would be enough for God's work through me.

Notes

All material quoted is used by permission.

1. Dr. and Mrs. Howard Taylor, *Hudson Taylor's Spiritual Secret* (Chicago: Moody Press, n.d.).

2. Ibid., p. 27.

3. Ibid., p. 31.

4. Colin M. Turnbull, *The Mountain People* (New York: Simon and Schuster, 1972), p. 292.

5. George Müller, *The Life of Trust* (New York: Thomas Y. Crowell Company, Pub., 1898), pp. 481-487.

6. Dr. and Mrs. Howard Taylor, *Hudson Taylor in Early Years. The Growth of a Soul* (London: The China Inland Mission, 1921), pp. 399,400.

7. Ibid., p. 32.

8. Ibid., pp. 314-316.

9. Ibid.

10. Taylor, *Spiritual Secret*, pp. 138,139.

11. Ibid.

12. Dr. and Mrs. Howard Taylor, *Hudson Taylor and the China Inland Mission* (London: China Inland Mission, 1958), p. 176.

13. Ibid., p. 204.

14. Ibid., pp. 290,291.

CHAPTER 5

Coping with Imperfection

An Insight into the Life of C.S. Lewis

"If I were to say what I really thought about pain, I should be forced to make statements of such apparent fortitude that they would become ridiculous if anyone knew who made them."[1] So wrote C.S. Lewis—scholar, teacher, former professor of Medieval and Renaissance English at Cambridge University—with an honesty about his inner feelings which could only characterize a person with great strength, a person strong enough to face his imperfection.

Again, showing himself as a man of contrasts, in speaking of the awesomeness of God, Lewis found his modern example in a child's story, *The Wind in the Willows*, where Rat and Mole approach Pan on the island:

" 'Rat,' he found breath to whisper, shaking, 'Are

you afraid?' 'Afraid?' murmured the Rat, his eyes shining with unutterable love. 'Afraid? of Him? O, never,
never. And yet—and yet—O Mole, I am afraid.' "[2]

Other theologians and philosophers might find their
examples only in the profound utterances of ancient
thinkers. Lewis could find depth of expression in the
simplicity of a child's story.

And so was the man Lewis; intellectual but human;
fearful yet honest; questioning yet believing; human
and imperfect like the rest of us. Yet in all of his strength
and at times weakness, he was honest enough to admit
to the imperfection which existed in himself and in the
rest of mankind. He could accept imperfection as just
that: neither virtue nor sin but human frailty. While
volumes have been written on C.S. Lewis, the intellectual, this strain of humanity which exists threads
throughout all of his writings and especially in his letters,
has been neglected.

Many misconceptions regarding imperfection and
sin persist about those who seek professional counseling. The least accurate and most unsophisticated mis-
conception is that a person consults a psychotherapist
when one is crazy. The idiocy of that statement is self
evident. More subtle is the idea in the mind of some
Christians that if people would just confess their sins
their problems would vanish. The idea being that sin is
at the root of most emotional problems. Unfortunately,
there are writers whose work reflects this erroneous
concept.

To the contrary, most people who consult me with
their emotional problems have difficulties which could
not accurately be labeled as sinful. Anxiety, depression,
sexual problems and the other difficulties which con-

front a counselor are certainly human imperfections, but hardly sins. The sin label not only makes the problem harder to bear because it adds the dimension of guilt, but also because it frequently hinders people from getting much needed help.

We are all imperfect. And when any imperfection becomes overwhelming we may need professional help. But what we do *not* need is theological put-downs, declarations of our sinfulness and inadequacy. "Be ye perfect," is a valid scriptural principle, but it is a call to wholeness, to completenes. It is not a denial of man's inevitable imperfection.

"You would like to know how I behave when I am experiencing pain, not writing books about it. You need not guess, for I will tell you; I am a great coward. But what is that to the purpose? When I think of pain—of anxiety that gnaws like fire and loneliness that spreads out like a desert, and the heartbreaking routine of monotonous misery, or again of dull aches that blacken our whole landscape or sudden nauseating pains that knock a man's heart out at one blow, of pains that seem already intolerable and then are suddenly increased, of infuriating scorpion-stinging pains that startle into maniacal movement a man who seemed half dead with his previous tortures—it 'quite o'ercrows my spirit.' If I knew any way of escape I would crawl through sewers to find it. But what is the good of telling you about my feelings? You know them already: they are the same as yours. I am not arguing that pain is not painful. Pain hurts. That is what the word means. I am only trying to show that the old Christian doctrine of being made 'perfect through suffering' is not incredible. To prove it palatable is beyond my design."[3]

Again, in relationship to anaesthetics Lewis describes the same fears:

"My reason is perfectly convinced by good evidence that anaesthetics do not smother me and that properly trained surgeons do not start operating until I am unconscious. But that does not alter the fact that when they have me down on the table and clap their horrible mask over my face, a mere childish panic begins inside me. I start thinking I am going to choke, and I am afraid they will start cutting me up before I am properly under. In other words, I lose my faith in anaesthetics."[4]

How many times do we fear pain before that pain occurs? I dreaded the phone call from the hospital announcing my father's death for weeks before it occurred. I feared it. Yet when the call came, I handled it. I didn't crumble, become hysterical or do any of the things my imagination had conjured up. I absorbed the shock for a little while, cooked breakfast for my mother and sister and helped with funeral arrangements. Often our anticipation and fear of physical and emotional pain outdoes its reality. But again, we are human and so we fear pain.

When questioned about suffering by one who suggested that a good God will not inflict pain, Lewis replied:

"What do people mean when they say 'I am not afraid of God because I know He is good?' Have they never even been to a dentist?"[5]

At the epitome of his life-pain, his grief over the death of Joy, his wife of three years, Lewis wrote not only of the pain he was feeling in handling this blow, but also of his doubt that he would ever totally recover:

"Getting over it so soon? But the words are ambiguous. To say the patient is getting over it after an operation for appendicitis is one thing; after he's had his leg off it is quite another. After that operation either the wounded stump heals or the man dies. If it heals, the fierce, continuous pain will stop. Presently he'll get back his strength and be able to stump about on his wooden leg. He has 'got over it.' But he will probably have recurrent pains in the stump all his life, and perhaps pretty bad ones; and he will always be a one-legged man. There will be hardly any moment when he forgets it. Bathing, dressing, sitting down and getting up again, even lying in bed, will all be different. His whole way of life will be changed. All sorts of pleasures and activities that he once took for granted will have to be simply written off. Duties too. At present I am learning to get about on crutches. Perhaps I shall presently be given a wooden leg. But I shall never be a biped again."[6]

In severe psychological pain the feeling that things will never be normal again is usual. A depressed lady who consulted me, after seeing several other therapists, kept saying, "I have a hard time coming here because I keep feeling that nothing can help." Lewis would have understood her feelings.

In a profoundly sympathetic view of the potential despair in everyone and himself, Lewis exclaims in his initial grief over Joy's death:

"They say an unhappy man wants distractions—something to take him out of himself. Only as a dog-tired man wants an extra blanket on a cold night; he'd rather lie there shivering than get up and find one. It's easy to see why the lonely become untidy; finally, dirty and disgusting."[7]

Of Niceness and Nastiness

And thus as he was realistic about himself, so he was equally aware of the frailties of mankind in general. His description of the questionable "niceness" of Christians in *Mere Christianity* says it well:

"We must, therefore, not be surprised if we find among the Christians some people who are still nasty. There is even, when you come to think it over, a reason why nasty people might be expected to turn to Christ in greater numbers than nice ones. That was what people objected to about Christ during His life on earth; He seemed to attract 'such awful people.' That is what people still object to, and always will. Do you not see why? Christ said 'Blessed are the poor' and 'How hard it is for the rich to enter the Kingdom,' and no doubt He primarily meant the economically rich and economically poor. But do not His words also apply to another kind of riches and poverty? One of the dangers of having a lot of money is that you may be quite satisfied with the kinds of happiness money can give and so fail to realize your need for God. If everything seems to come simply by signing checks, you may forget that you are at every moment totally dependent on God. Now quite plainly, natural gifts carry with them a similar danger. If you have sound nerves and intelligence and health and popularity and a good upbringing, you are likely to be quite satisfied with your character as it is. 'Why drag God into it?' you may ask. A certain level of good conduct comes fairly easily to you. You are not one of those wretched creatures who are always being tripped up by sex, or dipsomania, or nervousness, or bad temper. Everyone says you are a nice chap and (between ourselves) you agree with them. You are quite likely to believe that all this niceness is your own doing; and you may easily not feel the need for any better kind of goodness. Often people who have all these natural kinds of goodness cannot be brought to recognize their need for Christ at all until, one day, the natural goodness lets them down and their self-satisfaction is shattered. In other words, it is hard for those who are 'rich' in this sense to enter the Kingdom.

"It is very different for the nasty people—the little, low, timid, warped, thin-blooded, lonely people, or the passionate, sensual, unbalanced people. If they make any attempt at goodness at all, they learn, in double quick time, that they need help. It is Christ or nothing for them. It is taking up the cross and following—or else despair. They are the lost sheep; He came specially to find them. They are (in one very real and terrible sense) the 'poor': He blessed them. They are the 'awful set' He goes about with—and of course the Pharisees say still, as they said from the first, 'If there were anything in Christianity those people would not be Christians.'

"There is either a warning or an encouragement here for everyone of us. If you are a nice person—if virtue comes easily to you—beware! Much is expected from those to whom much is given. If you mistake for your own merits what are really God's gifts to you through nature, and if you are contented with simply being nice, you are still a rebel; and all those gifts will only make your fall more terrible, your corruption more complicated, your bad example more disastrous. The Devil was an archangel once; his natural gifts were as far above yours as yours are above those of a chimpanzee.

"But if you are a poor creature—poisoned by a wretched upbringing in some house full of vulgar jealousies and senseless quarrels—saddled, by no choice of your own, with some loathsome sexual perversion—nagged day in and day out by an inferiority complex that makes you snap at your best friends—do not despair. He knows all about it. You are one of the poor whom He blessed. He knows what a wretched machine you are trying to drive. Keep on. Do what you can. One day (perhaps in another world, but perhaps far sooner than that) He will fling it on the scrap-heap and give you a new one. And then you may astonish us all—not least yourself: for you have learned your driving in a hard school. (Some of the last will be first and some of the first will be last.)

" 'Niceness'—wholesome, integrated personality— is an excellent thing. We must try by every medical, educational, economic, and political means in our power to produce a world where as many people as possible grow up 'nice'; just as we must try to produce a world where all have plenty to eat. But we must not suppose that even if we succeeded in making everyone nice we should have saved their souls. A world of nice people, content in their own niceness, looking no further, turned away from God, would be just as desperately in need of salvation as a miserable world—and might even be more difficult to save."[8]

Most of us know that Christians are not all nice but find it a fact which is hard to admit to. We even know on a gut level that we are not always nice, and that is even harder for us to accept.

A Christian businessman confided in me that if he were to look at himself or other Christians for evidence of God he might have become discouraged and never known God. But because he focuses his attention on

God, his relationship with his maker is vigorous and real. Yet the concept of human frailty must never become a cop-out for sin. Gossip, pride, sexual sins, cheating, hate—all of these are not frailties but sins and roadbocks between the non-Christian and God. Lewis would be among the first to agree with this. Although he was not accepting of sin, he was a man of great brilliance and much humanness.

The Imperfection of Loneliness

A man of contrasts, C.S. Lewis was without a doubt one of the great intellectuals of the twentieth century. Yet in his letters he often wrote about simple things—his cats, his seemingly endless illnesses and some of his homely answers for those illnesses. He shocked *Time* magazine by stating that he did indeed *enjoy* monotony. He admitted his deep fear of poverty; yet after his death it became known that he had been giving away two-thirds of his income. He hated solitude; and perhaps partly because of that he endured the presence of an increasingly irascible housekeeper, Mrs. Moore, for years until her death. He preferred the problems of an incompatible living partner over those of solitude.

He had his routines, his after-dinner glass of port and his evenings with Tolkien when each read the other's manuscripts. Yet he could be spontaneous, as in his last travels with Joy just months before her death.

Lewis's awareness of his aloneness in this world came early as a child when he learned of his mother's death. It was the beginning of his facing, when he was still a child, his impending adultness. In his words:

"With my mother's death all settled happiness, all that was tranquil and reliable, disappeared from my life.

There was to be much fun, many pleasures, many stabs of joy; but no more of the old security. It was sea and islands now; the great continent had sunk like Atlantis.''[9]

Lewis never accepted his aloneness with feelings of comfortableness. Thus his fears, his closeness to his brother, his tolerance of Mrs. Moore, and his ecstasy and then deep sense of loss over his wife of three years are all understandable.

It is this combination of greatness and humanness in Lewis which is so encouraging to those of us who at times denigrate ourselves for being human.

Perspective on Human Value

Lewis had a gut respect for so-called ordinary people. In speaking of the "average" man Lewis commented:

"It seems that there is a general rule in the moral universe which may be formulated 'The higher, the more in danger.' The 'average sensual man' who is sometimes unfaithful to his wife, sometimes tipsy, always a little selfish, now and then (within the law) a trifle sharp in his deals, is certainly, by ordinary standards, a 'lower' type than the man whose soul is filled with some great Cause, to which he will subordinate his appetites, his fortune, and even his safety. But it is out of the second man that something really fiendish can be made; an Inquisitor, a Member of the Committee of Public Safety. It is great men, potential saints, not little men, who become merciless fanatics. Those who are readiest to die for a cause may easily become those who are readiest to kill for it.''[10]

Placing each person's value in proper perspective,

as dependent upon God for real value, Lewis further comments:

"Starting with the doctrine that every individuality is 'of infinite value' we then picture God as a kind of employment committee whose business it is to find suitable careers for souls, square holes for square pegs. In fact, however, the value of the individual does not lie in him[self]. He is capable of receiving value. He receives it by union with Christ. There is no question of finding for him a place in the living temple which will do justice to his inherent value and give scope to his natural idiosyncrasy. The place was there first. The man was created for it. He will not be himself till he is there. We shall be true and everlasting and really divine persons only in Heaven, just as we are, even now, coloured bodies only in the light."[11]

It was not that Lewis either glorified or denigrated any status of man. He simply saw the imperfection involved in all levels of mankind and realized that man's true potential for good lay only in his relationship with God. As an extension of that thought, Lewis believed that we are indeed our brother's keeper. As he put it, "There are no *ordinary* people." We are special to God and each other with sacred spiritual potential.

"Thus," says Lewis, "the load, or weight, or burden of my neighbour's glory should be laid daily on my back, a load so heavy that only humility can carry it, and the backs of the proud will be broken. It is a serious thing to live in a society of possible gods and goddesses, to remember that the dullest and most uninteresting person you talk to may one day be a creature which, if you saw it now, you would be strongly tempted to worship, or else a horror and a corruption such as you now meet, if at all, only in a nightmare. All day long we are, in some degree, helping each other to one or other of these destination. It is in the light of these overwhelming possibilites, it is with the awe and the circumspection proper to them, that we should conduct all our dealings with one another, all friendships, all loves, all play, all politics. There are no *ordinary* people. You have never talked to a mere mortal. Nations, cultures, arts, civilizations—these are mortal, and their life is to ours as the life of a gnat. But it is immortals whom we joke with, work with, marry, snub, and exploit—immortal horrors or everlasting splendours. This does not mean that we are to be perpetually solemn. We must play. But our merriment must be of that kind (and it is, in fact, the merriest kind) which exists between people who have, from the outset, taken each other seriously—no flippancy, no superiority, no presumption. And our charity must be a real and costly love, with deep feeling for the sins in spite of which we love the sinner—no mere tolerance or indulgence which parodies love as flippancy parodies merriment. Next to the Blessed Sacrament itself, your neighbour is the holiest object presented to your senses. If he is your Christian neighbour he is holy in almost the same way, for in him also Christ *vere latitat*—the glorifier and the glorified, Glory Himself, is truly hidden.''[12]

Were we to translate this viewpoint into actions in each of our lives, perhaps there would be little need for psychotherapists. Not, by the way, because needing therapy or counseling is sinful, but because loving our neighbor with all his imperfections, and his loving me back with all of mine, would be a good insurance policy against some of the problems which cause people to seek professional help.

Deceptive Reality

Imperfection can, at times, be deceptive, however. In spiritual matters our perception sometimes seems inadequate when compared to all that we perceive in the natural realm because we are so used to the natural. In our humanness we confuse reality with fiction, perfection with imperfection. Lewis gave an apt example:

"When I was a boy, gramophone records were not nearly so good as they are now. In the old recording of an orchestral piece you could hardly hear the separate instrument at all, but only a single undifferentiated sound. That was the sort of music I grew up on. And when, at a somewhat later age, I began to hear real orchestras, I was actually disappointed with them, just because you didn't get that single sound. What one got in a concert room seemed to me to lack the unity I had grown to expect, to be not an orchestra but merely a number of individual musicians on the same platform. In fact, I felt it 'wasn't the Real Thing.' This is an even better example than the former one. For a gramophone record is precisely a substitute, and an orchestra the reality. But owing to my musical miseducation the reality appeared to be a substitute and the substitute a reality."

Philosophically, Lewis explained his example:

"Things do look so very much as if our whole faith were a substitute for the real well-being we have failed to achieve on earth. It seems so very likely that our rejection of the World is only the disappointed fox's attempt to convince himself that unattainable grapes are sour. After all, we do not usually think much about the next world till our hopes in this have been pretty well flattened out—and when they are revived we not infrequently abandon our religion. And does not all that talk of celestial love come chiefly from monks and nuns, starved celibates consoling themselves with a compensatory hallucination? And the worship of the Christ child—does it not also come to us from centuries of lonely old maids? There is no good ignoring these disquieting thoughts. Let us admit from the outset that the psychologists have a good *prima facie* case. The theory that our religion is a substitute has a great deal of plausibility.

"Faced with this, the first thing I do is to try to find out what I know about substitutes, and the realities for which they are substituted, in general. And I find that I don't know so much as I thought I did. Until I considered the matter I had a sort of impression that one could recognize the difference by mere inspection if one was really honest—that the substitute would somehow betray itself by the mere taste, would ring false. And this impression was, in fact, one of the sources from which the doubts I mentioned were drawing their strength. What made it seem so likely that religion was a substitute was not any general philosophical argument about the existence of God, but rather the experienced fact that for the most of us at most times the spiritual life *tasted* so thin, or insipid, compared with the natural. And I thought that was just what a substitute might be expected to taste like. But after reflection, I discovered that this was not only not an obvious truth but was even contradicted by some of my own experience."[13]

Not long ago I experienced vividly this feeling of blurring—the real with the unreal—as I watched a play written by psychiatrist Viktor E. Frankl. Dr. Frankl had written this play shortly after his release from some of the worst Nazi concentration camps. It spoke movingly of the idea that life at all levels has meaning—even at the level of deep suffering. Meaning is the real substance of life. It is what makes life something more than superficial survival. As I sat in the audience I was moved by the reality of what I was seeing on stage. Truly the audience at that point was less real than the players. For the players were presenting life at its peak of meaning.

Related to this same idea that we do not always precisely identify reality, Lewis further explains how mere moods and simple circumstances often affect our spiritual beliefs and outlook:

"It is always assumed that the difficulties of faith are intellectual difficulties, that a man who has once accepted a certain proposition will automatically go on believing it till real grounds for disbelief occur. Nothing could be more superficial. How many of the freshmen who come up to Oxford from religious homes and lose their Christianity in the first year have been honestly *argued* out of it? How many of our own sudden temporary losses of faith have rational basis which would stand examination for a moment? I don't know how it is with others, but I find that mere change of scene always has a tendency to decrease my faith at first—God is less credible when I pray in a hotel bedroom than when I am in College. The society of unbelievers makes Faith harder even when they are people whose opinions, on any other subject, are known to be worthless.

"These irrational fluctuations in belief are not particular to religious belief. They are happening about all our beliefs all day long. Haven't you noticed it with our thoughts about the war? Some days, of course, there is really good or really bad news, which gives us rational grounds for increased optimism or pessimism. But everyone must have experienced days in which we are caught up in a great wave of confidence or down into a trough of anxiety though there are no new grounds either for the one or the other. Of course, once the mood is on us, we *find* reasons soon enough. We say that we've been 'thinking it over': but it is pretty plain that the mood has created the reasons and not *vice versa.*"[14] But there are examples closer to the Christian problem even than these.

Conflict of Faith and Sight

"There are things, say in learning to swim or to climb, which look dangerous and aren't. Your instructor tells you it's safe. You have good reason from past experience to trust him. Perhaps you can even see for yourself, by your own reason, that it is safe. But the crucial question is, will you be able to go on believing this when you actually see the cliff edge below you or actually feel yourself unsupported in the water? You will have no *rational* grounds for disbelieving. It is your senses and your imagination that are going to attack belief. Here, as in the New Testament, the conflict is not between faith and reason but between faith and sight. We can face things which we *know* to be dangerous if they don't look or sound too dangerous; our real trouble is often with things we *know* to be safe but which look dreadful. Our faith in Christ wavers not so much when real arguments come against it as when it *looks* improbable—when the whole world takes on that desolate *look* which really tells us much more about the state of our passions and even our digestion than about reality."[15]

Again Lewis does not condemn but he *gently* explains the sometimes irrational fluctuations which we all experience in our faith. Yet Lewis does not allow his reader to slump into the cop-out that because we are human God will understand. Because we cannot eradicate all our shortcomings and imperfections does not mean that we become passive about them. Here Lewis pushes the reader to examine his own motives when he says:

"For I am not sure, after all, whether one of the causes of our weak faith is not a secret wish that our faith should *not* be very strong. Is there some reservation in our minds? Some fear of what it might be like if our religion became *quite* real? I hope not. God help us all, and forgive us."[16]

Forgive us God does, for not only does He see our imperfections as just that but, also, while He wants us to grow into all we were ever meant to be, He forgives our mixed motives and is patient with our slowness.

Suzanne sat in my office, not long ago, sobbing because another Christian repeatedly told her she was incapable of ever changing. In truth, Suzanne has changed so obviously that even the social workers involved have been noticing the difference in her. She no longer becomes so depressed that she fails to feed her two-year-old child or shuts out the child's crying by covering her ears. Suzanne has become a good wife and mother; in fact, better than most. But her Christian friend fails to see this because she doesn't want to see it. In some smug way she feels more secure condemning her for past problems now gone, and which originally arose more from human imperfection than any sin. Truly, "God help us all, and forgive us!"

In talking of imperfection Lewis goes beyond him-self, beyond generalizations about people, and beyond theological discussion. In so doing he reaches down to some of the most practical issues people face. And at times he attacks these with a tremendous sense of humor.

In a letter to his brother Lewis discusses an incident in which he became involved. It is worth quoting exten-sively because of its rare humor, insight into human frailty, and his acceptance of all types of people. Ex-plains Lewis:

"I have a ludicrous adventure of my own to tell. Mme Balot is the widow of a M. Balot who died recently. She had been temporarily insane once during his lifetime; and tho' there was no serious fear of a relapse, her state of mind after his death . . . led most of her friends to keep an eye on her. Mrs. Moore [Lewis's housekeeper] went to see her pretty regularly. So did the heroine of my story, Mrs. Moreton . . . 'a brave little woman,' tho' it is not known what danger she ever had to encounter. She is a spiritualist, she weighs the babies of poor women, her business is universal benevolence.

"Well, the other night Mrs. Moore suddenly called me out of the dining room and said, 'Mrs. Moreton is here. She says that Mme Balot twice tried to commit suicide today. She has got a taxi here and wants me to go and see the doctor at the Warneford. We shall have to get a nurse for Mme Balot' . . . I stayed in the taxi while the two ladies went in to see the doctor . . . . They emerged at last with a Nurse Jackson and we started off for the Balots' house. But now the question was what to do? Madame would certainly refuse to have a strange young woman thrust upon her for the night for no

apparent reason . . . no one had any authority over her
. . . no doctor would certify her as insane . . . . Mrs.
Moreton said it was all perfectly simple. She would stay
hidden in the Balot garden all night. Nurse could be put
up in the bungalow of a stranger opposite to Madame's
house . . . . If only she [Mrs.Moreton] could have a *man*
with her, she confessed she would feel less nervous
about it. I began to wish I'd stayed at home; but in the
end of course I had to offer. No one raised the question
as to why the Nurse had been prevented from going to
bed in her hospital in order to be carried half a mile in a
taxi and immediately put to bed in another house totally
unconnected with the scene of action, where she could
not possibly be of the slightest use. The nurse herself,
who was possibly in some doubt as to who the supposed
lunatic might be, maintained a stupefied silence. I now
suggested as a last line of defence that nothing would be
more likely to upset Mme Balot than to find dim figures
walking about her garden all night; to which Mrs. Moreton replied brightly that we must keep out of sight and
go very quietly. 'We could put our stockings on outside
our boots, you know.' We were whispering outside a
house just down the street, and at this stage a window
opened overhead and someone asked me rather curtly
if we wanted anything, and if not would we kindly go
away. This restored to me some of the sanity which I was
rapidly losing, and I determined that whatever else happened, four o'clock should not find me 'with my stockings over my boots' in someone else's garden for fear
the owner might commit suicide, explaining this to a
policeman.

"I therefore ruled that we must keep our watch in
the road, where, if we sat down, we should be hidden

from the windows by the paling (and, I added mentally, would be open to arrest for vagabondage, not for burglary). Several neighbours had now turned up . . . to revel in the excitement and Mrs. Moreton (while insisting on the absolute necessity of letting no one know) gave each newcomer a full account of the situation . . . . I came home, drank a cup of tea, put on a greatcoat, took some biscuits, smokes, a couple of apples, a rug, a waterproof sheet, and two cushions and returned to the fatal spot . . . . Someone had had the rare good sense to leave some sandwiches and three thermos flasks, and I found the brave little woman actually eating and drinking when I arrived. Hastily deciding that if I was to lie under the obligations of a *man* I would assume his authority, I explained that we would be really hungry later on and authoritatively put a stop to that nonsense. . . .

"I settled down. There had been some attempt at moonlight earlier, but it had clouded over and a fine rain began to fall. Mrs. Moreton's feminine and civilian vision of night watches had evidently not included this. She was surprised at it. She was also surprised at its getting really cold; and most surprised of all to find that she was getting really sleepy . . . . If I could have been quit of her society I should have found my watch just tolerable—despite the misfortune of finding my greatcoat pockets stuffed with camphor balls which I flung angrily on the road, and then some hours later forgetting this and trying to eat one of the apples. The taste of camphor is exactly like the smell . . . . However, my story is over now, and when I have added that the crows had been 'tuning up for their unseasonable matins' a full half hour before any other bird squeaked (a fact of natural history which I never knew before) I may dismiss Mrs. Moreton from my mind . . . ."17

Search for the Perfect Setting

On a more specific level, most of us encounter problems or issues which in a way seem trivial or, if they seem great, our approach to them may appear so futile and ineffective that we hardly dare express our feelings for fear that others would laugh or not understand. Our approach to finding the right setting and the right time for our work can be like that. For instance, today I missed an airplane because of a flat tire. At first I was annoyed. I had an appointment in my home city, friends meeting me, and things to do at home before tomorrow's day in the office. Then I realized with delight that today I would be isolated in a strange town where I could have hour upon hour free to write. Yet the whole scene reminded me afresh of my frequent frustration over unfinished work. Another human frailty, if you please. Lewis has some very comforting thoughts on the subject:

"There are always plenty of rivals to our work. We are always falling in love or quarrelling, looking for jobs or fearing to lose them, getting ill and recovering, following public affairs. If we let ourselves, we shall always be waiting for some distraction or other to end before we can really get down to our work. The only people who achieve much are those who want knowledge so badly that they seek it while the conditions are sitll unfavourable. Favourable conditions never come."

Commenting further on work, Lewis writes:

"If I say to you that no one has time to finish, that the longest human life leaves a man, in any branch of learning, a beginner, I shall seem to you to be saying something quite academic and theoretical. You would be surprised if you knew how soon one begins to feel the shortness of the tether: of how many things, even in middle life, we have to say 'No time for that,' 'Too late now,' and 'Not for me.' But Nature herself forbids you to share that experience. A more Christian attitude, which can be attained at any age, is that of leaving futurity in God's hands. We may as well, for God will certainly retain it whether we leave it to Him or not. Never, in peace or war, commit your virtue or your happiness to the future. Happy work is best done by the man who takes his long-term plans somewhat lightly and works from moment to moment 'as to the Lord.' It is only our *daily* bread that we are encouraged to ask for. The present is the only time in which any duty can be done or any grace received."[18]

I read these comforting words and felt better about my own less than perfect planning. I too am learning that "Happy work is best done by the man who takes his long-term plans somewhat lightly and works from moment to moment 'as to the Lord.'"

Routine Prayer

In the matter of prayer Lewis writes in a letter a comment that should relax any Christian who demands a certain routine experience in his or her daily prayer life:

"We all go through periods of dryness in our prayers, don't we? I doubt . . . whether they are necessarily a bad symptom. I sometimes suspect that what we *feel* to be our best prayers are really our worst; that what we are enjoying is the satisfaction of apparent success, as in executing a dance or reciting a poem. Do our prayers sometimes go wrong because we insist on trying to talk to God when He wants to talk to us.

"Joy tells me that once, years ago, she was haunted one morning by a feeling that God wanted something of her, a persistent pressure like the nag of a neglected duty. And till mid-morning she kept on wondering what it was. But the moment she stopped worrying, the answer came through as plain as a spoken voice. It was 'I don't want you to *do* anything. I want to *give* you something; and immediately her heart was full of peace and delight.

"St. Augustine says 'God gives where He finds empty hands.' A man whose hands are full of parcels can't receive a gift. Perhaps these parcels are not always sins or earthly cares, but sometimes our own fussy attempts to worship Him in *our* way. Incidentally, what most often interrupts my own prayers is not great distractions but tiny ones—things one will have to do or avoid in the course of the next hour."[19]

Hang-ups and Moral Choices

Regarding psychological hang-ups Lewis was accepting of the very least up to the more severe. In his *Letters to an American Lady* he refers to her impending surgery with the words: "Fear is horrid but there's no reason to be ashamed of it. Our Lord was afraid (dreadfully so) in Gethsemane. I always cling to that as a very comforting fact." And that in essence is the very heart of C.S. Lewis and imperfection. He was much comforted by his Lord in the midst of the vicissitudes of life. God was not a club. Lewis reverenced and feared Him. Lewis knew his God too well to feel that He would not do anything but comfort His children who try so terribly hard at times to be perfect, and yet fail.

Perhaps in *Mere Christianity* Lewis expresses one of his clearest thoughts on psychological problems:

"When a man makes a moral choice two things are involved. One is the act of choosing. The other is the various feelings, impulses and so on which his psychological outfit presents him with, and which are the raw material of his choice. Now this raw material may be of two kinds. Either it may be what we would call normal: it may consist of the sort of feelings that are common to all men. Or else it may consist of quite unnatural feelings due to things that have gone wrong in his subconscious. Thus fear of things that are really dangerous would be an example of the first kind: an irrational fear of cats or spiders would be an example of the second kind. The desire of a man for a woman would be of the first kind: the perverted desire of a man for a man would be of the second. Now what psychoanalysis undertakes to do is to remove the abnormal feelings, that is, to give the man better raw material for his acts of choice: morality is concerned with the acts of choice themselves.

"Put it this way. Imagine three men who go to war. One has the ordinary natural fear of danger that any man has and he subdues it by moral effort and becomes a brave man. Let us suppose that the other two have, as a result of things in their subconscious, exaggerated, irrational fears, which no amount of moral effort can do anything about. Now suppose that a psychoanalyst comes along and cures these two: that is, he puts them both back in the position of the first man. Well it is just then that the psychoanalytical problem is over and the moral problem begins. Because, now that they are cured, these two men might take quite different lines. The first might say, 'Thank goodness I've got rid of all those doo-dahs. Now at last I can do what I always wanted to do—my duty to the cause of freedom.' But the other might say, 'Well, I'm very glad that I now feel moderately cool under fire, but, of course, that doesn't alter the fact that I'm still jolly well determined to look after Number One and let the other chap do the dangerous job whenever I can. Indeed one of the good things about feeling less frightened is that I can now look after myself much more efficiently and can be much cleverer at hiding the fact from the others.' Now this difference is a purely moral one and psychoanalysis cannot do anything about it. However much you improve the man's raw material, you have still got something else: the real, free choice of the man, on the material presented to him, either to put his own advantage first or to put it last. And this free choice is the only thing that morality is concerned with.

"The bad psychological material is not a sin but a disease. It does not need to be repented of, but to be cured. And by the way, that is very important. Human beings judge one another by their external actions. God judges them by their moral choices. When a neurotic who has a pathological horror of cats forces himself to pick up a cat for some good reason, it is quite possible that in God's eyes he has shown more courage than a healthy man may have shown in winning the V.C. [Victoria Cross]. When a man who has been perverted from his youth and taught that cruelty is the right thing, does some tiny little kindness, or refrains from some cruelty he might have committed, and thereby, perhaps, risks being sneered at by his companions, he may, in God's eyes, be doing more than you and I would do if we gave up life itself for a friend.

"It is as well to put this the other way round. Some of us who seem quite nice people may, in fact, have made so little use of a good heredity and a good upbringing that we are really worse than those whom we regard as fiends. Can we be certain how we should have behaved if we had been saddled with the psychological outfit, and then with the bad upbringing, and then with the power, say, of Himmler? That is why Christians are told not to judge. We see only the results which a man's choices make out of his raw material. But God does not judge him on the raw material at all, but on what he has done with it. Most of the man's psychological make-up is probably due to his body: when his body dies all that will fall off him, and the real central man, the thing that chose, that made the best or the worst out of this material, will stand naked. All sorts of nice things which we thought our own, but which were really due to a good digestion, will fall off some of us: all sorts of nasty things which were due to complexes or bad health will fall off others. We shall then, for the first time, see every one as he really was. There will be surprises."[20]

Learning to Love the "Others"

In the areas vital to Christian living, Lewis is not only practical but reassuring. How often we try to love and end up failing. To love those I find unlovable, I have discovered that I need to very honestly pray: "Lord, I don't love _____, but I am willing to have you love _____ through me." Then I have learned, I must *act* in love. Similarly Lewis says:

"But though natural likings should normally be encouraged, it would be quite wrong to think that the way to become charitable is to sit trying to manufacture affectionate feelings. Some people are 'cold' by temperament; that may be a misfortune for them, but it is no more a sin than having a bad digestion is a sin; and it does not cut them out from the chance, or excuse them from the duty, of learning charity. The rule for all of us is perfectly simple. Do not waste time bothering whether you 'love' your neighbour; act as if you did. As soon as we do this we find one of the great secrets. When you are behaving as if you loved someone, you will presently come to love him. If you injure someone you dislike, you will find yourself disliking him more. If you do him a good turn, you will find yourself disliking him less. There is, indeed, one exception. If you do him a good turn, not to please God and obey the law of charity, but to show him what a fine forgiving chap you are, and to put him in your debt, and then sit down to wait for his 'gratitude,' you will probably be disappointed. (People are not fools: they have a very quick eye for anything like showing off, or patronage.) But whenever we do good to another self, just because it is a self, made (like us) by God, and desiring its own happiness as we desire ours, we shall have learned to love it a little more or, at least, to dislike it less."[21]

Struggling with Impropriety

Another problem, that of modesty or chastity is so simply and acceptingly discussed that one wonders why so many of us have tried to put such issues in rigid boxes which have never really worked. According to Lewis:

"The Christian rule of chastity must not be confused

with the social rule of 'modesty' (in one sense of that word); i.e. propriety, or decency. The social rule of propriety lays down how much of the human body should be displayed and what subjects can be referred to, and in what words, according to the customs of a given social circle. Thus, while the rule of chastity is the same for all Christians at all times, the rule of propriety changes. A girl in the Pacific islands wearing hardly any clothes and a Victorian lady completely covered in clothes might both be equally 'modest,' proper, or decent, according to the standards of their own societies; and both, for all we could tell by their dress, might be equally chaste (or equally unchaste). Some of the language which chaste women used in Shakespeare's time would have been used in the nineteenth century only by a woman completely abandoned. When people break the rule of propriety current in their own time and place, if they do so in order to excite lust in themselves or others, then they are offending against chastity. But if they break it through ignorance or carelessness they are guilty only of bad manners. When, as often happens, they break it defiantly in order to shock or embarrass others, they are not necessarily being unchaste, but they are being uncharitable: for it is uncharitable to take pleasure in making other people uncomfortable. I do not think that a very strict or fussy standard of propriety is any proof of chastity or any help to it, and I therefore regard the great relaxation and simplifying of the rule which has taken place in my own lifetime as a good thing. At its present stage, however, it has this inconvenience, that people of different ages and different types do not all acknowledge the same standard, and we hardly know where we are. While this confusion lasts

I think that old, or old-fashioned, people should be very careful not to assume that young or 'emancipated' people are corrupt whenever they are (by the old standard) improper; and, in return, that young people should not call their elders prudes or puritans because they do not easily adopt the new standard."[22]

Lewis concludes with the line which, while not compromising with sin, sets the stage for real acceptance of other people with their, at times, varying standards. "A real desire to believe all the good you can of others and to make others as comfortable as you can will solve most of the problems."

As a little girl I was not allowed to attend the theater. I can still remember sneaking off at times to see a Walt Disney movie. But I only half enjoyed it. I sat nervously near the aisle and watched the lights over the exit doors on either side of the theater. As long as they were still burning I knew God had not come and taken His own away, leaving me. The conditioning was deep, for until a few years ago theaters still made me edgy.

While some movies are sinful because of what they portray, I'm sure that my childhood was not corrupted by Walt Disney. Indeed the fantasy and, at times, pathos of those stories enriched those years. And in the whole area of ethics, that which is not directly sinful must be relegated to the individual conscience of the believer, which leaves room for imperfection to creep in. For example, there is the matter of temperance—how much TV we watch or how many movies we see, if we can find that many good ones! These are things we must work out. But "God knows our situation; He will not judge us as if we had no difficulties to overcome. What matters is the sincerity and perseverance of our will to overcome them."[23] If God does not judge, then neither should we judge ourselves or anyone else for imperfection.

I frequently counsel people who come from good Christian backgrounds and have turned against God because people in the church judged them where God would not have. Or, they were rightly judged, but without love.

Someday we who are Christians will have to give a reason for those so turned away. And in the same way others will have to account for the hurt they caused their brother who didn't turn away but who suffered under their intolerance. In the meantime, we who know our own imperfection can be more accepting of ourselves and of others because of God's love and acceptance of us. For God has perfect balance in contrast to our lack of it.

Enroute to Perfection

In the words of C.S. Lewis: "On the one hand, God's demand for perfection need not discourage you in the least in your present attempts to be good, or even in your present failures. Each time you fall He will pick you up again. And He knows perfectly well that your own efforts are never going to bring you anywhere near perfection. On the other hand, you must realise from the outset that the goal towards which He is beginning to guide you is absolute perfection; and no power in the whole universe, except you yourself, can prevent Him from taking you to that goal."[24]

Continues Lewis: "When a man turns to Christ and seems to be getting on pretty well (in the sense that some of his bad habits are now corrected), he often feels that it would be natural if things went fairly smoothly. When troubles come along—illness, money troubles, new kinds of temptation—he is disappointed. These things, he feels, might have been necessary to rouse him and make him repent in his bad old days; but why now? Because God is forcing him on, or up, to a higher level: putting him into situations where he will have to be very much braver, or more patient, or more loving, than he ever dreamed of being before. It seems to us all unnecessary: but that is because we have not yet had the slightest notion of the tremendous thing He means to make of us.

"I find I must borrow yet another parable from George MacDonald. Imagine yourself as a living house. God comes in to rebuild that house. At first, perhaps, you can understand what he is doing. He is getting the drains right and stopping the leaks in the roof and so on: you knew that those jobs needed doing and so you are not surprised. But presently he starts knocking the house about in a way that hurts abominably and does not seem to make sense. What on earth is He up to? The explanation is that He is building quite a different house from the one you thought of—throwing out a new wing here, putting on an extra floor there, running up towers, making courtyards. You thought you were going to be made into a decent little cottage: but He is building a palace. He intends to come and live in it Himself."[25]

In our own efforts we can be nothing but imperfect. As human beings, God still loves us, imperfect as we are. And, in the words of C.S. Lewis:

"If we let Him—for we can prevent Him, if we choose—He will make the feeblest and filthiest of us into a god or goddess, a dazzling, radiant, immortal creature, pulsating all through with such energy and joy and wisdom and love as we cannot now imagine, a bright stainless mirror which reflects back to God perfectly (though, of course, on a smaller scale) His own boundless power and delight and goodness. The process will be long and in parts very painful; but that is what we are in for. Nothing less. He meant what He said."[26]

Notes

All material quoted is used by permission.

1. C.S. Lewis, *The Problem of Pain* (New York: The Macmillan Company, © 1943, 1945, 1952), p.9.

2. Ibid., p. 18.

3. Ibid., p. 105.

4. C.S. Lewis, *Mere Christianity* (New York: Macmillan Publishing Company, Inc., 1964), p. 109.

5. C.S. Lewis, *A Grief Observed* (New York: The Seabury Press, 1963), p. 36. © 1961 by N.W. Clerk.

6. Ibid., p. 43.

7. Ibid., pp. 8,9.

8. Lewis, *Mere Christianity*. pp. 180-182.

9. C.S. Lewis, *Surprised by Joy* (New York: Harcourt Brace Jovanovich, Inc., 1956), p. 21.

10. C.S. Lewis, *Reflections on the Psalms* (New York: Harcourt Brace Jovanovich, Inc., 1964), p. 28.

11. C.S. Lewis, *The Weight of Glory* (Grand Rapids: William B. Eerdmans Publishing Company, 1965), pp. 40,41. © by the executors of the Estate of C.S. Lewis, 1967.

12. Ibid., pp. 14,15.

13. C.S. Lewis, *Christian Reflections* (Grand Rapids: William B. Eerdmans Publishing Company, 1974), p. 39.

14. Ibid., p. 42.

15. Ibid., p. 43.

16. Ibid.

17. W.H. Lewis, ed., *Letters of C.S. Lewis* (New York: Harcourt Brace Jovanovich, Inc., 1975), pp. 118-120. © 1966 by W.H. Lewis and executors of C.S. Lewis.

18. Lewis, *Weight of Glory*, p. 52.

19. C.S. Lewis, *Letters to an American Lady* (Grand Rapids: William B. Eerdmans Publishing Company, 1967), p. 73.

20. C.S. Lewis, *Mere Christianity*, pp. 84-86.

21. Ibid., p. 116.

22. Ibid., pp. 88,89.

23. Ibid., p. 92.

24. Ibid., p. 172.

25. Ibid., p. 174.

26. Ibid., pp. 174,175.

CHAPTER 6
Coping Within an Eternal Perspective

It was in Mexico that I realized most fully—and for the first time in my life—that a whole host of situations in life cannot be eradicated. As a child, for example, going to a doctor meant to me that one would be automatically well. Then a little friend of mine died from polio, even though her father was a doctor. When I was in my teens I was hurt in an automobile accident. As I waited for the ambulance, I remember a kind man bending down saying, "We never think that this can happen to us." And I didn't think it could. But it did. And I kept having flash thoughts that this had to be just a nightmare and I would soon wake up.

Yet throughout my early life I held on tenaciously to

the notion that a problem could always be conquered, eliminated, done away with. Injustice could be abolished if we worked hard enough. The impossible just took a little longer, as the saying goes. Disillusionment came at times when my theory failed, but I rationalized that with a little more work the next attempt would be successful.

Somehow in Mexico the beginning of realism broke through upon my thinking. It's not that I became less idealistic. For more than ever I believe that God can indeed do the impossible and there is no person alive in whom God cannot perform miracles.

But now my idealism is at last becoming temperate. Each time I stayed for any amount of time in that tropical climate I was totally defeated by the onslaught of mosquitos and my allergy to them. Coming from Southern California, where heat is eliminated by air conditioned cars, homes and stores, I now found myself in a much hotter climate grasping gratefully for purified ice cubes. I looked around and saw hunger that was not satisfied, animals that suffered without a Society for the Prevention of Cruelty to Animals, death unsoftened by funeral homes, and lives which could not be dramatically altered.

In the United States we have easy answers for many problems. The government subsidizes our proverty, takes care of us, to a degree, in old age. We have instant food, microwave ovens, immediate news coverage from all points in the world, sophisticated medical treatment and, in general, many comforts that most of mankind has never even dreamed of. Yet even for us, and at times especially for us, the basic problems of mankind like loneliness, physical pain, depression, anxiety, can still not be eradicated. To believe otherwise is to be disillusioned. To accept this fact as reality is to begin the process of coping.

Many times we mistakenly believe that greatness implies the eradication of problems. In the lives of Charles Spurgeon, Amy Carmichael, Hudson Taylor and C.S. Lewis we have clear examples that such is not the case. They coped. They grew. But for them, like us, pain as well as pleasure ebbed and flowed throughout their lives.

So-called victorious Christian living is not found in the eradication of problems. It is to be found in handling problems with all the resources we can gather of physical well being, emotional growth, and the all sufficiency of God.

It is a profound relief to know that we are in good company with such an illustrious group of people who in spite of their problems and hurt in this life learned to cope with life and became truly great, both in the eyes of man and of God.

Hebrews 12:1 reads: "Since we have such a huge crowd of men of faith watching us from the grandstands, let us strip off anything that slows us down or holds us back, . . . and let us run with patience the particular race that God has set before us" (*TLB*). Amy Carmichael wrote that she believed that this "huge crowd of men of faith" are literal witnesses. That from heaven they literally observe us, support us, encourage us. Much theological debate has centered around this verse; but I, for one, agree with Miss Carmichael. And my "particular race" that God has set before me has been focused and motivated by the thought that I have the support of such people. Their encouragement would not be so great, however, if they had in their lifetimes eradicated all pain and problems. They would not have been real. But because they were great, yet mortal, I garner inspiration and hope from their lives.

Tonight I walked down by the ocean and watched the tide as it moved relentlessly in and out over the smooth shoreline. The softness of the rocky beach was evidence of the fact that the tide always does go back and forth. It never stays and it never fails to return. So it is with our feelings. Painful and joyful they do not stay. They leave, they return. And part of the gracefulness of maturity is to know this fact. For no matter how painful things become the feelings do not remain. Nor can they be eradicated. For pain in one form or another returns. But again, only for a time. But what does remain forever is the One who is God and the host of heavenly beings who surround us with love and care.

That Presence does not guarantee the eradication of need, whether the need be emotional, spiritual or material. But He does guarantee that needs can be met; that cope-ability can be provided.

As Hudson Taylor began the impossible task of evangelizing inland China, he was told: "You will be forgotten . . . With no committee or organization before the public, you will be lost sight of in that distant land. Claims are many nowadays. Before long you may find yourselves without even the necessaries of life!"

"I am taking my children with me," was the quiet answer, "and I notice it is not difficult to remember that they need breakfast in the morning, dinner at midday and supper at night. Indeed, I could not forget them if I tried. And I find it impossible to think that our heavenly Father is less tender and mindful of His children than I, a poor earthly father, am of mine. No, He will not forget us!"[1]

Hudson Taylor's God is our God. He alone, along with heaven's forces, remains the ultimate source of all coping!

Note

All material quoted is used by permission.
1. Dr. and Mrs. Howard Taylor, *Hudson Taylor's Spiritual Secret* (London, Philadelphia, Toronto: China Inland Mission, 1949).